DEDICATION

This work is dedicated to:

Rick Gieniec and Scot Cerulli,
growth-oriented students of life
from whom I have learned.

Gale and Ruth Swartz,
for parental support on all levels.

Elaine Ainsworth,
for her research on the older adult learner
and her contributions to that area of study.

TABLE OF CONTENTS

Overview 8

Background
  Definition of Accelerated Learning 10
  Characteristics of Accelerated Learning 12
  History of Accelerated Learning 18
  Results of Accelerated Learning
    Implementation 22

Brain/Mind Research Findings
  The Brain: A Working Model 26
  The Limbic System: Stress and Learning .. 32
  Left and Right Cerebral Hemispheres 40
  Brain Waves and Their Characteristics 54
  The Holographic Brain................................... 60

Methods
  Brain Dominance and Learning Styles:
    An Overview 76
  Imagery 92
  Peripheral Visual Aids 108
  Learning Affirmations.................................... 114
  Subliminals 122
  Music.. 126
  Relaxation 138

4-Step Self Study Process
  Creating a Learning Environment............... 142
  Relaxation Exercises 148
  Active Study 160
  Review and Reinforcement 166

Health Care Training Model
  Health Care Training Model: An Overview 172
  Creating a Stress-Free Learning
    Environment 176
  Relaxation Exercises 182
  Orchestrated Learning:
    Active and Passive 184

    Elaboration and Reinforcement 190
    Experiential Learning 192
    Special Needs of the Older Adult Learner 196
Appendices
    Appendix A – Brain Dominance
        Occupational Profiles 206
    Appendix B – Brain Dominance
        Occupational Profiles: Narrative
        Descriptions 210
    Appendix C – Format Guidelines for
        Creating a Text 214
    Appendix D – Permission Form: Learning
        Affirmation Audio Subliminals 218
    Appendix E – Musical Learning Notes 220
    Appendix F – New Age Music 224
    Appendix G – Active Learning Narrative
        Dialogue: An Example 226
Sources
    Resources 240
    References 244

TABLES

TABLE 6.1 – Stress	35
TABLE 10.1 – Brain Dominance: Definition of Terms	89
TABLE 10.2 – Learning Styles Represented by the Specialized Modes of the Four Quadrants	91
TABLE 11.1 – Evolutionary Development of the Major Components of the Triune Brain	96
TABLE 13.1 – Affirmations	116
TABLE 22.1 – Introduction Exercise: Ball Toss	180

FIGURES

FIGURE 5.1 – The Triune Brain	28
FIGURE 5.2 – The Limbic System	30
FIGURE 6.1 – Reactions to Stress	34
FIGURE 7.1 – Left and Right Hemisphere Specialization	42
FIGURE 7.2 – The Lobes and Sensory Areas of the Human Brain	44
FIGURE 7.3 – Left and Right Hemisphere Specialization	50
FIGURE 8.1 – The Four Brain Wave Patterns	56
FIGURE 9.1 – Holographic Photograph	62
FIGURE 9.2 – A Typical Nerve Cell	64
FIGURE 9.3 – Detail of a Synapse	66
FIGURE 9.4 – Synaptic Transmission	68
FIGURE 10.1 – The Interconnected Brain System Quadratic Model	80
FIGURE 10.2 – The Whole Brain Quadratic Model	82

FIGURE 10.3 — Herrmann Brain Dominance Profile 84
FIGURE 10.4 — Example of Dominance Occupational Profile 86
FIGURE 10.5 — Whole Brain Teaching and Learning Model 88
FIGURE 11.1 — Book Format, Example for Left/Right Note-Study System 100
FIGURE 11.2 — Left/Right Note-Study System 102
FIGURE 11.3 — Mind Map 106
FIGURE 17.1 — The Four-Step Accelerated Learning Self-Study Process 144
FIGURE 18.1 — Diaphragmatic Breathing 152
FIGURE 20.1 — Subsequent Review 170
FIGURE 21.1 — The Accelerated Learning Health Care Training Cycle 174

Overview

Information overload. Chronic stress. A quickening pace. Rapid change. A plethora of research data produced by our technological society.

Given the current accelerated rate of information generation, people need accelerated, innovative learning methods in order to keep pace. Reams of national studies indicate that current educational systems are sliding farther and farther behind information processes. Traditional methods of incorporating and learning the new information being generated just won't do.

This text proposes a system of learning that takes into account the current accelerated pace of information generation and that combines current brain/mind research regarding man's ability to assimilate information quickly with study skills and memory/mnemonic devices. The result is an accelerated learning system that can be applied to any field of study. Resources for additional information and training workshops in accelerated learning techniques are listed in Section #35.

Although the accelerated learning process can be applied to students of all ages, this text is geared to the adult learner, especially Sections #21 through #27, which apply accelerated learning methods to formal training and education, and Section #27, which incorporates the research findings related to older adult learners into the self-study process. Additionally, the wording of the text is supraliminally associated with the adult learner.

The structure of this text is intended to foster memory retention by combining the author's developed accelerated learning format with the copyrighted center index and bullet system of Essential Medical Information Systems, Inc. publishing company. Research indicates that retention and learning of textual material is enhanced by the specific placement of material within a book, ie, illustrations on left-hand pages and narrative descriptions on right-hand pages. Wherever possible, this format has been followed in this text.

Research also indicates that the greater the number of senses employed in the learning process and the greater their involvement, the better and faster the learning. To this end, the text's examples and illustrations are presented in second person in an attempt to engage the reader and to tap his senses. To enhance reader involvement even further, the text is worded as positively as possible; the term "participant," for example, often replaces the term "student," and "facilitator" often replaces "teacher."

By using these techniques in its presentation, this innovative text attempts to "practice what it preaches." The result should provide the reader with immediately applicable accelerated learning skills that will enhance learning, memory recall, and, as a by-product, health maintenance.

#1 Definition of Accelerated Learning

Definition

Accelerated learning is the art and science of:
- Encoding information into the neuroanatomical brain and holographic brain/mind
- Retrieving encoded information
- Applying learned abilities so that they may most effectively and efficiently access and use the:
  - Conscious
  - Paraconscious
  - Subconscious

Application of Accelerated Learning Skills

Accelerated learning skills can be applied to all areas of endeavor. Examples of specific uses of skills in specific areas include:

1. For business and industry, health care, and government:
   - Verbal memorization
   - Rate learning
   - Cognitive education (intellectual skills)
   - Psychomotor abilities, including:
     - Fine and gross motor dexterity
     - Eye-hand coordination
     - Strength
     - Agility
   - Affective education (changes in and/or development of values, interests, and attitudes)

Applications of skills may occur in such settings as:
- On-the-job training
- Formal training programs, such as those for:

- Leadership and motivation
- Assertiveness, stress management, management and supervision
- Sales and marketing
2. Formal education, including continuing education programs and workshops:
   - Homework/test preparation
   - Presentations to colleagues and students
3. Self-improvement:
   - Hobbies (for learning and recalling instructional information)
   - Formal courses and workshops
   - Informal instruction (reading)

References: 43

#2 Characteristics of Accelerated Learning

The principles of many educational, psychological, business, industrial, and medical technologies have been incorporated into accelerated learning methodology, including:
- Multifaceted learning
- Whole-brained (holistic) learning
- Multidimensional learning
- Integration of pedagogical and andragogical learning
- Timing and reinforcement
- Tension states of learners
- Simultaneous learning
- Multidisciplinary learning

Multifaceted Learning

Learning occurs in the cognitive, psychomotor, and affective domains. Cognitive learning is associated with the recognition and recall of knowledge and intellectual skills, such as reciting the bones in the hand, verbalizing organizational rules and regulations, problem-solving, and acquiring and using language.

Psychomotor learning pertains to skills used in performing specific tasks; some educators believe that this learning occurs in the manipulative or motor (movement) domain. Examples of psychomotor skills include handwriting, driving a car, operating machinery, and playing a violin.

Affective learning refers to development of and changes in attitudes, interests, appreciations, values, and intra- and interpersonal adjustments. Examples include changing behaviors (eg, from aggression to assertiveness), developing relationships, and reconsidering religious values.

Whole-Brain (Holistic) Learning

Accelerated learning involves the application of at least one and as many as four recognized thinking and learning styles (see Section #10) and the utilization of both left and right cerebral hemispheric functions (see Section #7).

Multidimensional Learning

The methods employed in accelerated learning access all levels of consciousness: the conscious, paraconscious, and subconscious. Consciousness includes everything that the learner is aware of mentally, physically, and emotionally and involves sensory integration.

Paraconsciousness includes information that is on the threshold of conscious awareness, ie, a dim awareness of the internal (mind, body, emotions) and external environment. For example, a person may be working quietly and suddenly become aware that the neighbor's lawn mover has been turned off. For that awareness to occur, the person had to be cognizant of the mower's noise initially; the cognizance that the lawn mower was in operation is in the paraconscious realm.

Subconsciousness involves those physical, mental, and emotional activities that occur in the realm below the conscious and paraconscious.

Integration of Pedagogical and Andragogical Learning

Pedagogy (Greek *agogus*, meaning guide) is the art and science of teaching children, (Greek *paid*, meaning child), and andragogy is the teaching of adults (Greek *aner*, meaning adult).

Pedagogical learning is characterized by:
- Teacher-centered instruction, in which stu-

dents learn only the material presented to them
- Objectives and instructional methodology determined by teachers

Andragogical learning is characterized by:
- Student-centered instruction and intrinsic motivation. Adults are self-directed when the subject area matches the skills they:
  - Have a desire to learn
  - Are required to know in order to get and keep a specific job
  - Must have for actual performance of a specific job
  - Must have before further learning can take place, ie, is a basis for additional learning to be built upon
- The perception that adults bring life experiences and cognitive perceptions to the learning situation that serve as building blocks or conceptual links (associations) to aid cumulative learning
- The allowance of different individual approaches to learning; approaches vary because attitudes, values, life experiences, and perceptions vary from person to person

Learning can be enhanced by integrating pedagogical and andragogical methods.
- Pedagogical methods include:
  - Parables
  - Imagery
  - Games
  - Music
  - Humor and laughter
  - Toys (puppets, Lincoln logs, erector sets, poster boards)

- Andragogical methods include but are not limited to:
  - Lecture
  - Question and answer
  - Discussion
  - Socratic questioning

Timing and Reinforcement

In order for long-term retention to take place, learned knowledge and skills must be used as quickly as possible, after their initial acquisition, and reinforcement mechanisms must be incorporated into the learning process.

Tension States of Learners

For optimal learning, students should balance the opposing states of relaxation and alertness, by focusing on the material to be learned yet being relaxed while learning it. If students are too stressed and anxious, information will register but not be retained; if they are too relaxed, attention, concentration, and focus will diminish.

Simultaneous Learning

Accelerated learning processes employ various methods simultaneously because the brain absorbs stimuli simultaneously, using all levels of consciousness concurrently. While reading, for example, a person may be aware of physical sensations and movements, eg, heartbeat, breathing, and other sounds (conscious and paraconscious) and be reminded of a past event and its associated emotions (conscious) simultaneously. Though the conscious focus is on the daydreaming, the person paraconsciously registers the information being read.

Because the brain assimilates all activities simultaneously, it is important that teachers and trainers be aware of the impact that environment has on learning and create environments for participants that are conducive to learning.

Multidisciplinary Learning

Methods utilized in accelerated learning (see Sections #10 through #16) are derived from various fields and disciplines. Examples are:

Relaxation methods, derived from:
- Psychology
- Psychoneuroimmunology (interrelationships of brain, mind, and body)
- Yoga and meditation traditions

Music methods, derived from:
- Music therapy
- Music genres
- Music behavioral medicine

Affirmations, derived from:
- Humanistic psychology
- Meditation traditions

Imagery methods, derived from:
- Mnemonics
- Psychoneuroimmunology
- Education/training

Peripherals, derived from:
- Education/training

Subliminal methods, derived from:
- Marketing and advertising
- Psychohypnosis

Brain dominance methods, derived from:
- Neuroanatomy
- Neurophysiology
- Neuropsychology

References: 27, 35, 43

NOTES

#3 History of Accelerated Learning

3.

In the early 1960s, Bulgarian Dr. Georgi Lozanov, a medically-trained psychotherapist, experimented with methods to improve the health care of his patients. He had studied Eastern yoga and meditation and believed in the power of the mind to influence physiological processes.

Following a basic yoga principle that deep states of relaxation ease emotional anxiety and physiological stress, Lozanov combined the principles and techniques of meditation, relaxation, verbal rhythmic intonation/cadences, breathing exercises, imagery, and music (research confirms that the human body naturally synchronizes with musical rhythms) to aid patients' pain control and healing, and integrated them with traditional medical treatment. As a result, he and others were consistently able to accelerate the healing process.

Lozanov discovered a major spin-off benefit of his study: patients' memory increased considerably as they experienced reduced stress and accelerated healing. The study of this benefit became Lozanov's life work. He reasoned that, if memory was enhanced by these methods, then learning could also be enhanced and accelerated by their use.

Lozanov and others believed that the brain acts as a vast sponge, absorbing all perceptions, stimuli, and information received. But he also believed, as did researchers in the Soviet Union, Europe, and the West, that human beings utilize only 10 percent of their brain capacities; research of neurology confirms this, indicating that a vast amount of learning potential never gets "tapped."

Canadian neurosurgeon at the Montreal Neurological Institute, Dr. Wilder Penfield, discovered stored yet forgotten memories in epileptic patients and found that, through electrical stimulation of certain parts of the brain, his patients could create "playback recall" of previous conversations, long-forgotten events, and senses associated with each.

Lozanov felt that his methods could help everyone tap into unused portions of their brains for more effective and efficient learning.

Suggestopedia and Suggestology

Lozanov termed the capability of associative recall *hypermnesia*, more simply defined as supermemory. Immersed in the culture and traditions of his country (including the political realities of living in an Eastern Bloc country), he developed a two-part system of learning to access and utilize hypermnesia, he called this system:

- Suggestology, the art and science of suggestion

and

- Suggestopedia, the active implementation of suggestology

Lozanov and his trained associates applied suggestology to the field of education, initially to the teaching of foreign language and later to the instruction of science and mathematics courses. Language instructors incorporated into their teaching methods such techniques as:

- Speaking in rhythmic cadences such as:
  - Slowing the rate of presentation of unfamiliar content
  - Synchronizing speech patterns with specific musical rhythms

- Speaking in short phrases and word clusters
- Vocal intonation
- Playing background music (especially Baroque and classical selections)
- Breathing and relaxation exercises
- Self-imaging
- Motivational therapy
- Affirmation

To this combination of methods, Lozanov added the techniques of pedagogy and andragogy in order to create a relaxed learning atmosphere. (Pedagogical techniques help to make learning fun; in this regard, Lozanov coined the term infantalization, the creation by the instructor of a childlike environment for the assimilation of any learning.)

Lozanov's Results
General

The positive results of Lozanov's methods cut across all demographic and economic distinctions.

Educational

Soon, educational results consistently replicated the clinical results found earlier in health care. Based on these findings, the 1966 Bulgarian Ministry of Education in Sophia created the Institute of Suggestology, which incorporated Lozanov's suggestology with other holistic, whole-brain educational methods, with the goal of enabling learners to tap into the unused reserves of the brain.

Lozanov's method consistently demonstrated that learning the vocabulary of a foreign language could be accelerated by as much as 5 times, with as much as 50 percent retention (without intensive reinforcement) after one year.

Health Care

Participants experienced reduced stress and tension during learning and were freed from the headaches they experienced prior to training.

References: 35, 43

#4 Results of Accelerated Learning Implementation

Results similar to Lozanov's (see Section #3) were replicated in the Soviet Union and Europe. Gradually, Lozanov's proposed educational methodologies made their way to North America. As the "movement" spread, others modified Lozanov's system and/or incorporated other techniques into it.

Over the years, the names of these learning systems have changed. Because of the political, "big brother" overtones of the term suggestology, nomenclature for Suggestopedic learning has evolved into such terms as Superlearning™, supermemory, OptimaLearning™, and accelerated learning (the term used throughout this text).

Currently in the U.S., accelerated learning techniques are being applied to business, industry, and health care training, as well as secondary and elementary school systems and some higher educational institutions (see Section #35 for organizations offering training in these learning techniques). Results of such studies made in health care and educational/training fields are summarized below.

Results in Health Care

Three critical components of accelerated learning—music, imagery, and relaxation—have been used for several decades in the treatment of health care patients. Their effectiveness has been under scientific investigation during the last several years; some of the studies have been compiled and published in textbook form.

Results in Education/Training
Instructors

Instructors trained in and using accelerated learning techniques can expect to achieve any or all of the following results when teaching:

- Because learning is accelerated and, thus, requires less time than traditional education methodologies, instructors may use that extra time as they choose, including:
  - Using an equivalent amount of time but covering a greater amount of material
  - Covering the same amount of material but in less time; this option reduces training time and costs of education
  - Using the extra time for:
    - Experiential learning
    - Reinforcement
    - Skills development
    - Students' enhancement of long-term recall
- Learning environments that enhance students' relaxed yet alert states

Students

Students whose instruction was based on techniques of accelerated learning can expect to achieve:

- Enhanced initial learning and long-term recall
- Reduced-stress learning environments (relaxed yet alert)
- The beneficial by-product of improved health associated with reduced stress

References:
  General: 27, 35, 43

  Health Care: 1, 4, 5, 7, 8, 10, 14, 15, 20, 21, 32, 33, 35, 36, 40, 41, 44

  Education/Training: 10, 11, 12, 18, 36, 44

  Resources: (See Section 35)
    Health Care: 14, 17
    Education/Training: 15, 18

NOTES

#5 The Brain: A Working Model

As humanity has evolved over the eons, so has the brain. Rather than being pictured as an efficient and effective computer whose processes and components are intact from the moment of inception, the brain should be thought of in architectural and/or archeological terms.

The brain is the architect for itself. Never static, it is ever evolving, adding new physiological functions (architectural structures) as needed for immediate survival and health maintenance of the species. Architecturally, the brain can be seen as a house, the exterior of which is the skull. This house contains many rooms and extensive closets and shelving. These rooms seem to be superimposed upon one another, with all the rooms linked through vast networks of electrical wiring. All parts of all rooms perform their different functions simultaneously, and all of the activity occurs within the house rather than outside it. Endless stimuli (guests) come and go, some of which have made themselves so at home that they seem to take up residence and leave only after months or years.

The architectural brain builds, modifies, and rebuilds itself in accordance with the physical, mental, and emotional growth and development of the human species.

The Triune Brain

The brain also can be seen in terms of an archeological dig, with layers superimposed upon one another. The model of the triune brain, developed by Dr. Paul MacLean, chairman of the National Institute for Mental Health's Laboratory for

Brain Evolution and Behavior, especially lends itself to this analogy. In this model, the brain is divided into three major components (Figure 5.1):
- The human brain
- The mammalian brain
- The reptilian brain

The Human Brain

An archeological "dig" of the brain would first uncover the neocortex, or human brain. This layer of the brain is the most recent of its evolved parts, occurring approximately 50 million years ago. Also termed the cortex and "thinking cap," this thin (about one-eight inch), enfolded layer of gray matter covers the surface of the cerebrum and makes up about 80 percent of the brain's total gray matter. If the cortex were unfolded and spread out, it would be about the size of a newspaper page.

As the hub of the human species' developed rational abilities, the cortex is the architect of the home, performing, perfecting, and noting those functions that make people uniquely human, ie:
- Thinking
- Making decisions
- Perceiving the past, present, and future
- Organizing external and internal environments
- Speaking
- Hearing
- Remembering
- Learning new methods of coping, adopting, and adapting

FIGURE 5.1 – **The Triune Brain**

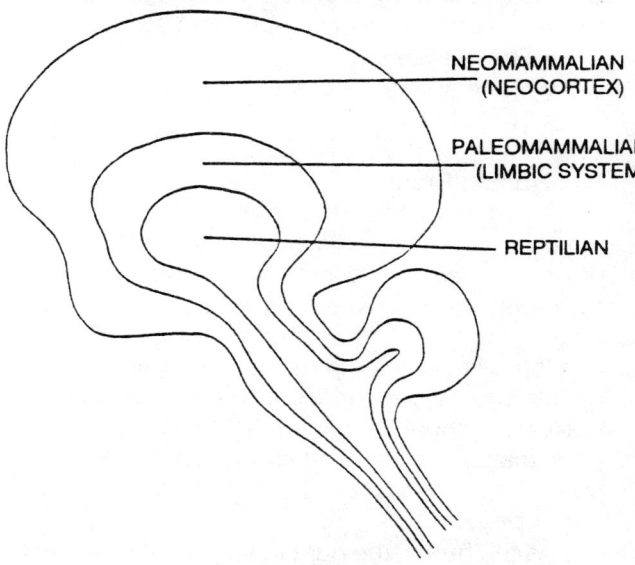

Herrmann N: The Creative Brain. Lake Lure, NC: Brain Books, 1988. Reprinted with permission by the Ned Herrmann Group, Applied Creative Services, Ltd.

The Mammalian Brain

Beneath the cerebrum lies the mammalian brain, so termed because its same structure is found in all land mammals. This part of the brain most likely evolved 200 to 300 million years ago when the species evolved from a sea into a permanent land species.

The mammalian brain contains the *limbic* system (Latin, meaning bordering or hemming in), which consists of two, almost concentric curved rings, each connected to the cerebrum's left and right hemispheres (see Section #7) and to each

other via the hippocampal commissure (Figure 5.2). The limbic system affects learning and physical and emotional health by serving three critical functions (see Section #6):
- Physical (body) maintenance
- Emotional stability
- Transference of information into memory storage and from short- to long-term memory

The Reptilian Brain

Lying below the limbic system is the ancient reptilian brain, which evolved more than 500 million years ago. Physiologically, this component of the brain sits atop the spinal cord and consists of two major parts:
- The matrix of the brain stem
- The reticular activating system (RAS)

It is the brain stem that gives this component of the human brain its reptilian title because its structure resembles that of a reptile's brain.

At the center of the brain stem lies the RAS, a core of neural tissue. The RAS is the brain's physical basis for consciousness and, as such, is the alarm or watchguard of the brain, sending the necessary impulses to the neocortex to keep human beings awake and alert.

Nerve impulses, or messages, are sent throughout the body from sensory receptors through the RAS via the spinal cord at a rate of 100 million per second, with a few hundred filtered through various components above the brain stem. The human mind requires only a few of these few hundred for consciousness. Sleep occurs when stimulation of the RAS or brain stem slackens; coma (loss of consciousness) occurs when stimulation is obstructed, as in injury to the brain stem.

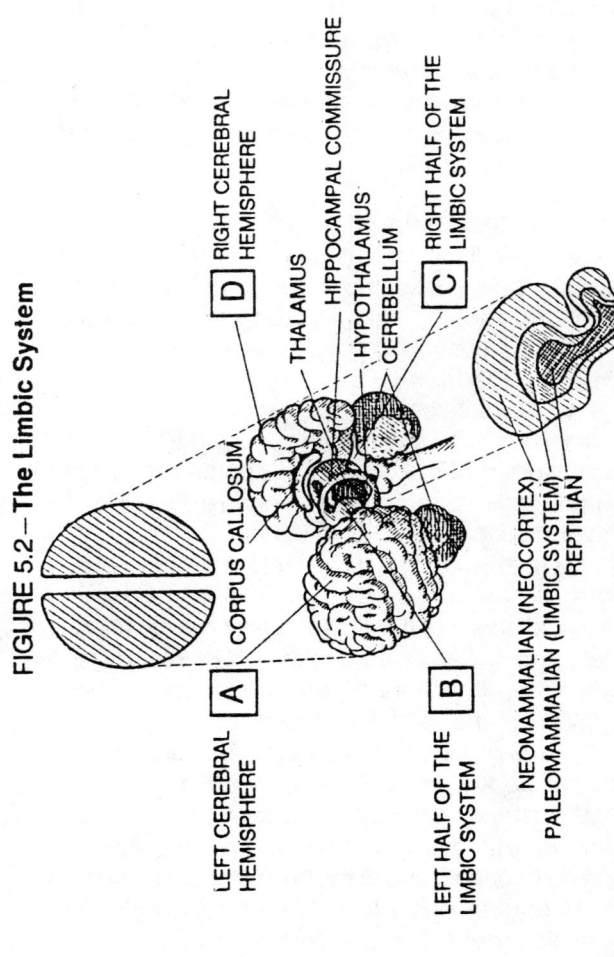

FIGURE 5.2 — The Limbic System

Herrmann N: The Creative Brain. Lake Lure, NC: Brain Books, 1988. Reprinted with permission by the Ned Herrmann Group, Applied Creative Services, Ltd.

The RAS continually sifts through the stimulations and messages received from the sensory receptors, selecting and sending to the conscious mind only those that are essential or unusual or that warn of danger. While a person may be peripherally aware of many sensory stimulations, conscious concentration is limited, sequentially, to one sensation at a time.

Research has discovered that the RAS also regulates *habituation*, a process in which the RAS alerts the conscious mind to a sensory novelty, and the neocortex, recognizing the stimulus (memory recognition), directs the RAS to halt its alerting action. At this point, the RAS perceives the stimulus as familiar, and the stimulus becomes peripheral. Peripherally, the person may be aware of the on-going stimulus and disregard the sensation until it ceases, at which time the consciousness becomes aware, through the RAS, of a "new" novelty, the cessation of that stimulus.

References: 19, 22, 25, 34

#6 The Limbic System: Stress and Learning

As stated in Section #5, the limbic system serves three functions:
- Physiological maintenance
- Emotional stability
- Information transference

6. Physiological Maintenance

Within the limbic system is the *hypothalamus* (about the size of a pea). The hypothalamus and limbic system together regulate:
- Eating
- Drinking
- Waking
- Sleeping
- Body temperature
- Hormonal balances
- Sexual drive
- Heart rate
- Blood pressure
- Blood sugar levels

Research has revealed that the hypothalamus also is directly involved in the regulation of the immune system and directs the activity of the pituitary gland, which produces the chemicals and hormones that are carried throughout the body's cellular structure and are thus critical to the immune system and to health.

The two center rings of the limbic system enclose upon the thalamus; the thalamus is connected to the limbic system by a mass of nerves. The thalamus acts as the main relay station, analyzing stimuli and passing information (in the form of sensory impulses) through the nerves to other parts of the brain, including the neocortex.

These physiological functions of the limbic system help to maintain *homeostasis*, ie, a stable environment for the body.

Emotional Stability

In addition to acting as the physical thermostat, the limbic system also serves as the *emotional thermostat* and is often referred to as the emotional brain. In 1937, neuroanatomist James Papez of the National Institute of Health postulated that the brain's neuroanatomical circuitry was involved in both thought and emotion. Subsequent electrochemical research validated Papez's theory and demonstrated that the limbic system helps to maintain emotional homeostasis of such paired emotions as:

- Rage/fear
- Pleasure/pain (reward/punishment)
- Tension/relaxation (see Section #2 — relaxed yet alert balance of accelerated learning)
- Expectation/actuality
- Fight/flight response

Without such balance, the human being would experience emotional extremes.

Stress directly impacts the limbic system (Figures 6.1 and 6.2), with the hypothalamus coordinating the fight or flight response, ie, the physical and emotional responses to a stressor. The limbic system, via the hypothalamus, readies the body to deal with a crisis (real or imagined) by stimulating the pituitary gland to secrete adrenocorticotropic hormone (ACTH). ACTH, in turn,

FIGURE 6.1 – **Reactions To Stress**

Stress activates hypothalamus to stimulate other glands

Hypothalamus stimulates pituitary gland to release adrenocortotrophic hormones (ACTH) into the bloodstream (to the adrenal gland)

Bronchial tubes open to permit deeper breathing

Heart beats faster and contracts strongly

Blood sugar rises, digestive system slows

Adrenal glands release norephinephrine to the nervous system and more ACTH to the bloodstream

Blood pressure rises, muscles contract, blood vessels dilate to allow greater blood flow but surface blood vessels contract, blood clots quickly if surface blood vessels are injured

TABLE 6.1 – **Stress**

STRESS

The positive
or negative
physiological response
(end result)
within the body.
This response
is created
by
physical, mental, and/or emotional
stimuli.
These stimuli
are in the
external (outside the body)
and/or
internal (within mind and/or body)
environments,
and interact with
the emotions.

Copy R.G. Swartz & Associates
Management Impact Skills

triggers the adrenal cortex to pump adrenaline and to release chemicals that initiate the metabolism of proteins and fats into sugar, activities which provide the body with the energy and strength required for working through a crisis situation.

Additional physical reactions to a crisis include:
- Increased heart rate
- Elevated blood pressure
- Increased metabolic rate
- Muscle tension
- Release of blood clotting factors and enzymes
- Increased perspiration

These physical and chemical reactions literally pump the body up in response to a stressor, poising it for action. Such responses have enabled the human species to survive and evolve. Indeed, some researchers contend that the major purpose of the brain is survival and health maintenance.

In a complex society, crises may manifest themselves in less than concrete ways and create a fight or flight response that never shuts down. An animal's limbic system returns the body to physical and emotional homeostasis as soon as a threat is dealt with and/or removed. However, due to his sense of past, present, and future time, man retains the memory of a crisis even after a stressor is physically removed from the environment or mentally (intellectually) removed from the consciousness.

Man constantly collects and emotionally retains such experiences as rush hour traffic, job stresses, daily duties, and major life crises, creating for himself long-term, chronic stress. If left unchecked, this stress can lead to heart and other diseases and suppression of the body's immune system.

Information Transfer

Interconnected with man's ability to think, ie, cognitive/intellectual mental language ability (thinking), and to think within time parameters, is *learning*: the registration of stimuli and their recall (memory). Some researchers do not distinguish between learning and memory, seeing them as interconnected processes; but learning and memory, though interconnected, do differ. *Memory* is the process of the recall of data which has already been learned and encoded within the brain; thus, learning must precede recall.

For the conscious mind, the recall of a memory (data) involves two distinct processes:
- The attempt to initiate a recall of data from storage banks; if successful, the attempt results in recalled data
- A recognition that the memory (data recalled) corresponds to the recall attempt

The limbic system aids learning and memory retention by serving two functions, ie:
- Directing information, processed by the brain, into appropriate memory storage areas distributed (apparently) through the brain
- Transferring information from short- to long-term memory

The hippocampus, a component of the limbic system, has been discovered to play an important role in initial learning and short-term memory. Short-term memory consists of two types:
- Very short-term, lasting for a second or less—As the brain perceives information from the senses, it briefly retains the stimulus

- Short-term, lasting from several seconds to one minute — The capacity of human attention limits the amount of information a person can focus on

Because the brain continually attempts to simplify the external environment, only a fraction of the information received is actually retained in memory. Very short-term memory works just long enough for the conscious mind to grasp information, after which information may be peripherally held for several seconds (but no longer than a minute) in short-term memory. Research has shown that the average individual can hold only about seven new items of information in short-term memory. An intriguing question is whether peripheral material vanishes from short-term memory forever or is stored (see Section #3).

For information to be remembered, ie, placed in long-term memory, it must be reinforced. This may be accomplished by repeating it several times, writing it down and repeating it, or using memory cues, mnemonics (see Section #11), or other memory aids. Through the conscious effort of reinforcement, new information is encoded into the brain for later retrieval.

Research indicates that memories, even sensory memories, are integrated in the limbic system. For example, one component of the limbic system, the rhinencephalon (Greek, meaning "nose brain"), is believed to be concerned with the sense of smell. Certain smells evoke vivid imagery (see Section #11) and associated memories, which are activated in the rhinencephalon because odors directly impact the memory through sensory imagery.

References: 4, 16, 19, 20, 22, 25, 28, 34, 36, 47

NOTES

#7 Left and Right Cerebral Hemispheres

The study of the human brain (cerebrum and cortex) and mind remains a scientific frontier, especially regarding their respective roles in learning and memory. Questions that arise in such study include:
- Is the mind the physiological, neurological brain?
- Where is it located within the brain?
- What is the seat of consciousness? Where is it?
- Is the mind a component of, or a vehicle for, the soul?
- How do learning and remembering occur?
- How do children learn their native languages so rapidly and effectively?
- What accounts for children's ability to learn language?
- Where is memory stored in the brain?

The Cerebral Hemispheres

Relative to body size, the human brain, from the neocortex to the end of the brain stem, is the largest brain of all land animals. The cerebrum, including its surface (the cortex), is divided into two hemispheres. These are interconnected by a bridge called the corpus callosum, the largest fiber pathway found in the brain; it contains approximately 300 million nerve fibers and is approximately four inches long.

The left and right rings of the limbic system (see Section #6), are also interconnected by a nerve fiber pathway called the *hippocampal commissure*, and each ring contains neurological connections to its respective cerebral hemisphere.

Consequently, the cerebral human brain is strongly linked to the mammalian brain, and each hemisphere is strongly interconnected to the other (Figure 7.1).

Cerebral Hemisphere Lobes

One of the brain's primary functions is regulation of the body (see Section #5). The cerebral hemispheres aid in this function, a critical point being that each hemisphere physiologically controls the side of the body opposite it.

Each hemisphere is subdivided into four lobes (Figure 7.2), each having a left and right half. From anterior to posterior, these are:
- Occipital lobe
- Parietal lobe
- Temporal lobe
- Frontal lobe

The Occipital Lobe

The occipital lobe, or visual cortex, deals exclusively with vision. Visual information is sent from both eyes to the visual cortex, where it is analyzed for:
- Orientation
- Position
- Movement

Physical damage to either side of the occipital lobe can result in blindness, though the rest of the brain's complex visual system can remain intact and unaffected.

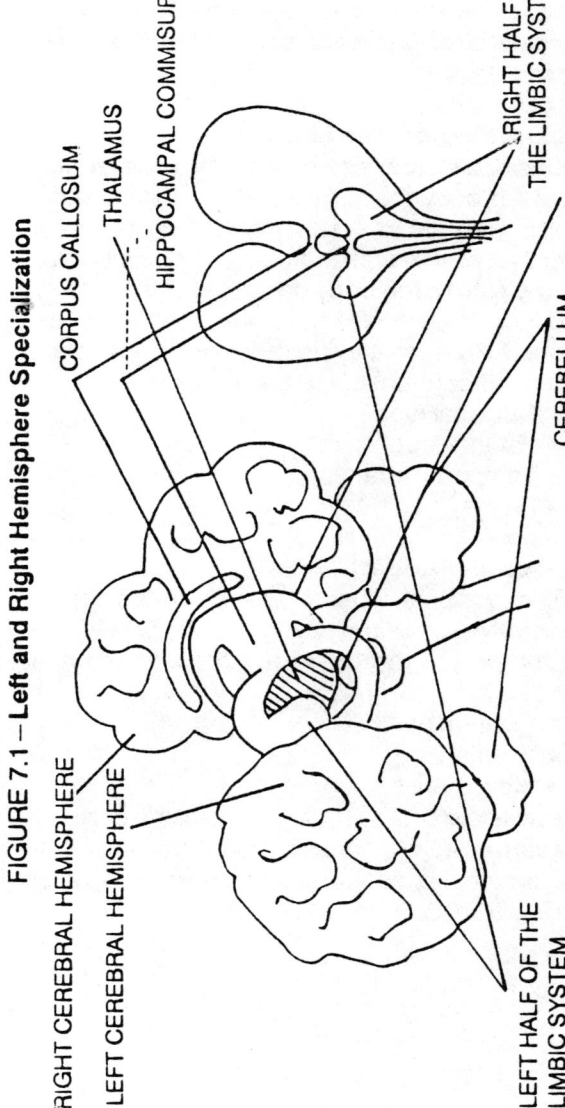

FIGURE 7.1 – Left and Right Hemisphere Specialization

Herrmann N: The Creative Brain. Lake Lure, NC: Brain Books, 1988. Reprinted with permission by the Ned Herrmann Group, Applied Creative Services, Ltd.

The Parietal Lobe

Each side of the parietal (Latin, meaning "forming the sides") lobe is located toward the posterior of each cerebral hemisphere. It is in this lobe that the brain forms perceptions of the environment. Research indicates that the parietal lobe also aids in the formation of letters into words and words into thoughts.

Damage to either side of the parietal lobe can result in *agnosia* (a state of being unaware, a lack of sensory-perceptual ability to recognize objects). Manifestations of damage to one side are seen on the opposite side of the body; for example, damage to the right parietal lobe may result in the loss of knowledge of the existence of the left side of the body, so that the afflicted person may fail to recognize the need to groom or dress that side of the body.

Located near each parietal lobe, though they are not lobes themselves, are *somatic* or physical sensory areas. These areas consist of:

- The sensory cortex, which receives information about body position, muscles, exertion of pressure, and touch
- The motor cortex, which controls movement

The Temporal Lobe

Most scientific knowledge of the functions of the temporal lobe is derived from the study of people who have suffered physiological damage to this area of the brain. The temporal lobes, located near the temples, have the functions of:

- Hearing
- Perception
- Memory

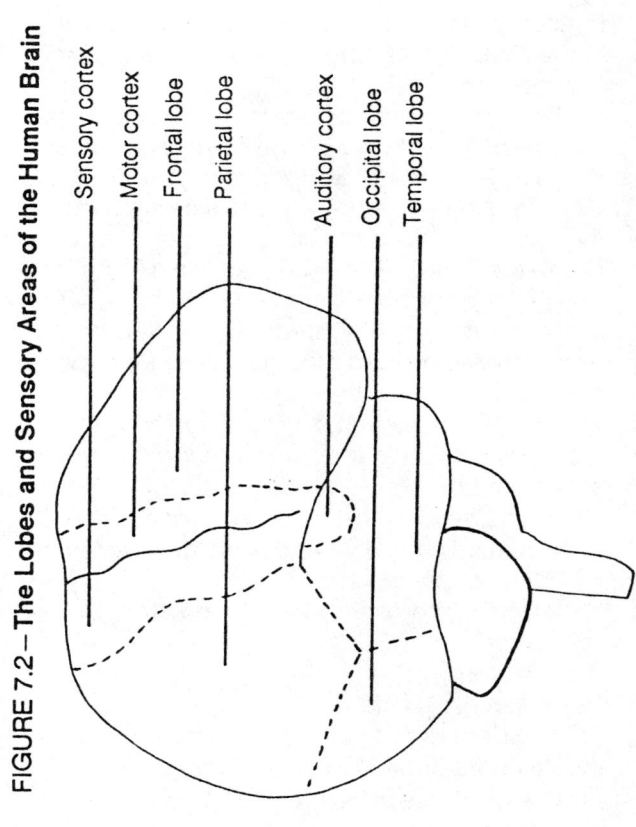

FIGURE 7.2 – The Lobes and Sensory Areas of the Human Brain

Hearing

The temporal lobes contain the auditory cortex. About the size of a poker chip, the auditory cortex is essential for the detection of changes in sound frequencies and for the orientation of a sound's source.

Damage to either side of the temporal lobe may result in severe difficulty in interpreting sound, especially spoken language. Damage to the left lobe can result in *aphasia* (the loss of language, ie, the loss of the ability to organize word sounds and word sequences into meaningful sentences).

Perception

The right temporal lobe deals with perception. Damage to this lobe results in impaired performance of spatial tasks, such as the ability to draw.

Memory

Surgical patients have been known to report experiencing a sense of being in two places at the same time if the temporal lobe (either side) is stimulated electrically during the operation. They report sensations connected to a past experience, recalling the event while simultaneously remaining consciously aware of their present surgical experience.

The Frontal Lobe

The frontal lobe, the largest of the four lobe pairs, is situated just behind the forehead. These lobe pairs are critically significant to the functions of:

- Emotions (the frontal lobe is physiologically connected to the limbic system)
- Cognition (planning, decision-making, analysis, implementation, etc.)

Damage to or removal of (lobotomy) either side of the frontal lobe results in a person's:
- Becoming distracted by irrelevant sensory stimuli
- Inability to:
  - Perform cognitive skills
  - Adapt to new situations
  - Focus attention
  - Plan ahead

Knowledge of frontal lobe functions and of the results of lobe damage was gained during the period from 1942 to 1954 in which mental disorders were treated by psychosurgery. Noted emotional responses of lobotomy patients included changes in behavior, such as:
- Lowered moral standards
- Loss of social sense or of an awareness of and sensitivity to others
- Emotional incontinence (a termed used by researcher Walter Freeman to describe the uncontrolled expression of a wide range of emotional responses over a short period of time)

During this time Russian neuropsychologist Alexander Luria became acutely aware of the functions of the frontal lobes:
- Emotional response — Luria speculated that those with intact frontal lobes would experience emotions directly opposite the emotions of those whose lobes had been damaged or removed. Specifically they would:
  - Possess high moral standards
  - Be aware of and have sympathy and empathy for others
  - Be able to control their emotions and maintain emotional balance or homeostasis

- Intellectual and memory recall, planning, and implementation of a plan — Luria found the frontal lobe to be critical to:
  - The awareness of time (past, present, and future)
  - The awareness of events
  - Planning and implementation of events within time frames

To perform these functions, the brain's activity resembles the following scheme (these events actually occur simultaneously, though they are outlined in sequence form):

- Attention — Each frontal lobe calls attention or focused awareness to a situation
- Activation — The entire brain is activated to deal with the situation
- Filtering — The brain filters out irrelevant material in order to focus on the situation at hand
- Memory recall — The frontal lobes search their memory stores for similar, relevant past experiences and successful reactions to the situation at hand, matching the memory recalled with the recall attempt (see Section #6). The lobes also organize bits of memory information into an entire remembered image
- Analysis — The situation is identified, and the information regarding the present and recalled events is analyzed, synthesized, and classified
- Planning — Once an analysis is made, a goal is determined and strategies for attaining that goal are planned. The temporal lobes become involved at this point, since planned strategies occur in time frames

- Implementation — The planned strategy is physically acted upon via communication of information from the frontal lobe to the brain's motor centers
- Evaluation — The frontal lobe:
  - Compares the results of the implemented plan to:
    - The analysis of the situation
    - The selected goals
    - The implementation plan
  - Draws conclusions about the success of the plan

Left and Right Cerebral Hemispheres: Lateral Specialization

Although each cerebral hemisphere contains sides of the same lobe type and each have somatic areas, the left and right hemispheres have specialized functions. Such lateral specialization, or lateralization, evolved relatively recently (3 to 4 million years ago) and is perhaps the last major development in the brain's evolution.

The cortex covers the surface of both hemispheres, performing functions that enhance man's ability to adapt to his environment. It is within the cortex that man manifests his uniqueness as a thinking, speaking, decision-making species.

Lateral specialization was discovered through the study of patients who either underwent removal of one hemisphere or whose corpus callosum (the network of nerve fibers that connect the hemispheres) had been severed for the control of epileptic seizures. During the 19th century, patients who experienced damage to parts of their brains were also studied. Study results indicated that:

- Damage to certain parts of the left hemisphere impedes:
  - Speech
  - Verbal memory
  - Mathematical functioning
  - Language ability
  - The sense of time
- Damage to certain parts of the right hemisphere impedes:
  - Visual and tactile tasks
  - Depth and movement perception
  - Visuo-spatial orientation

Studies of non-damaged, functioning hemispheres by Robert Ornstein and others conclusively corroborate the theories of specialization.

Left Hemisphere Specialization

Researchers have discovered that the specific functions of the left cerebral cortical hemisphere (Figure 7.3) include:
- Processing information within a time frame, ie, time orientation
- Processing events sequentially
- Verbal and written language skills
- Logic and rationalization
- Mathematics and sciences
- Analysis
- Convergent thinking skills
- Awareness of cause-and-effect relationships
- Regulation of functions of the right side of the body
- Emotions of happiness associated with perceived pleasant experiences

FIGURE 7.3 – **Left and Right Hemisphere Specialization**

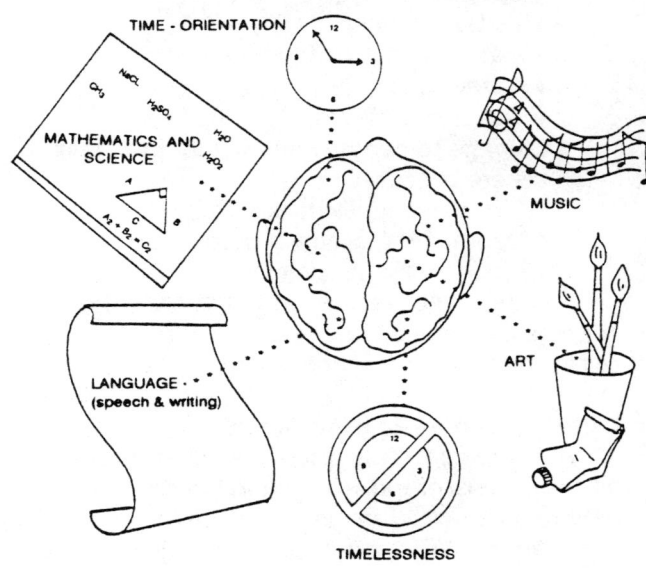

Right Hemisphere Specialization

Research has disclosed that the specific specializations of the right cerebral hemisphere (Figure 7.3) include:
- Processing information in a timeless state
- Processing events simultaneously
- Visuo-spatial orientation
- Art, imagery, and pattern awareness
- Music
- Holistic perceptions and synthesis of information
- Divergent thinking skills

- Regulation of functions of the left side of the body
- The emotion of anger
- Intuitive abilities

Integrations of Left and Right Hemisphere Functions

The two cerebral hemispheres are complementary rather than competitive. Their coordinated activities are enhanced by the brain's physiology through:

- The corpus callosum, which allows the hemispheres to share learning and memory and unifies attention and awareness. The corpus callosum is 10 percent larger in females than males, allowing for increased rapid transit of neural impulses between the hemispheres; females literally can move ideas back and forth more quickly than males
- The hippocampal commissure, which connects the two halves (rings) of the limbic system (Figure 7.1), enabling the limbic system to coordinate activities

For complex problem-solving, the left hemisphere analyzes components of a problem (convergent thinking), while the right derives alternative solutions to it (divergent thinking). To make a decision, the derived solutions are compared to the initial problem (left brain) and proposed solutions are evaluated in terms of their relationships to the overall situation (right brain).

An example of the complementary functions of the two hemispheres involves musical ability. Music is a precise art, involving mathematic, analytical, and technical composition skills, yet it is an art which evokes emotions and imagery; thus, both hemispheres of the brain are required for musicianship.

Implications for Accelerated Learning

Because the complementary and coordinated functions of the brain's two hemispheres are natural phenomena, individuals have at their disposal a superior resource which can be used to enhance learning. Learning can become highly efficient and effective when the resource of specialized brain functions is tapped (see Section #3) and integrated into educational activities (see Section #4).

References: 16, 19, 22, 25, 29, 34, 42

NOTES

#8 Brain Waves and Their Characteristics

One of the instruments used to determine hemispheric lateralization (see Section #7) of the brain is the electroencephalograph (EEG), which records the electrical voltage generated by the brain via electrodes attached to the skull's surface. Because the specialized cortex lies directly below the skull on the surface of the cerebrum, the brain's activities can be monitored easily.

The EEG results in a print-out, or brain print, of electrical brain wave action (brain wave patterns), which can be read to determine the efficiency of the natural abilities and functions of the brain. Among the brain's natural abilities is situational functioning, ie, its ability to call into action specialized regions (lobes) to deal with specific situations.

Regions not required in a given situation remain in a resting state, exhibited on the EEG by slow brain wave patterns. This phenomenon indicates that the brain actually conserves energy. Brain waves (electrical stimulations) are generated by the cortex's approximately 100 billion neurons (nerve cells), and the brain is capable of generating an electrical charge of approximately 10 watts. Conservation of energy, then, is important to efficient brain activity.

Hemispheric Specialization and Brain Wave Patterns

The brain emits four types of brain waves (Figure 8.1), each producing a wave band according to its cycles-per-second frequency of impulses:
- Beta – 13 to 30 cycles per second
- Alpha – 8 to 13 cycles per second

- Theta — 4 to 8 cycles per second
- Delta — 0.05 to 4 cycles per second

Brain wave activity varies throughout the day and night, producing any of the patterns at one time or another; some researchers term these different activity stages "altered states of consciousness." As the environment changes, neural activity changes (due to situational functioning); as neural activity changes, brain wave activity changes within each cerebral hemisphere.

The print-out of brain wave activity demonstrates hemispheric lateralization. During a given task, the hemisphere that is relatively quiet in terms of electrical activity shows less brain wave stimulation on the EEG than that of the hemisphere called into action. For example, the EEG records and demonstrates a predominance of alpha brain waves from the right hemisphere and less from the left during the performance of a task which requires left hemispheric functions, such as writing a letter. The pattern is reversed when a spatial task, such as arranging a set of colored blocks to match a given pattern, is performed, because the task requires right hemisphere function.

Researchers regard the alpha brain wave pattern as an indication of a slowing or lessening of information processing. In the letter-writing task, it is the left hemisphere with the predominance of beta brain wave activity, indicating a fast pace of mental activity involving information processing; in the spatial task, it is the right hemisphere with beta wave predominance. Researchers have used brain wave activity information to demonstrate hemispheric lateralization.

FIGURE 8.1 The Four Brain Wave Patterns

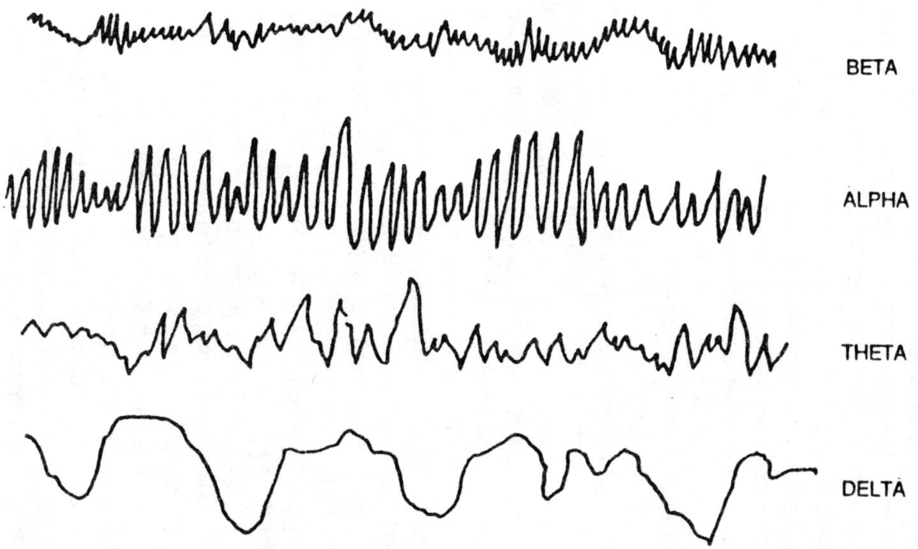

BETA

ALPHA

THETA

DELTA

The Four Brain Waves and Their Characteristics

During the last several decades, research of brain wave patterns as they relate to the fields of health, music, education, and psychology (including sleep research) has resulted in the identification of specific characteristics associated with each brain wave pattern:

Beta:
- Mental concentration
- Focus
- Activity by the hemisphere specialized to deal with a given situation
- Stress, anxiety, tension, hyperactivity
- Light or active REM sleep, vivid dreaming

Alpha:
- Increased relaxation
- Decreased stress
- Increased learning ability
- Increased capability for physical healing, manifesting itself by:
  - Lowered heart rate and blood pressure
  - Decreased oxygen consumption and respiratory rate
- Ability for prolonging focused, alert concentration
- Deeper sleep realm than that exhibited in beta

These characteristics imply an optimal state for learning, wellness, and healing.

Theta ("super alpha"):
- Enhancement of characteristics associated with alpha

Delta (slow, steady waves):
- Deep sleep, difficulty in awakening
- Sleepwalking
- Sleeptalking
- Bedwetting

References: 19, 25, 34, 35, 36

NOTES

#9 The Holographic Brain

Among the areas under scientific study of the brain are the phenomena of learning and memory. Questions abound about these functions of the brain:

- Is memory stored in speech areas of the brain?
- Or, are memories dispersed widely throughout the brain and allocated (via the limbic system) to the specific brain region whose lateralized functions (see Section #7) are associated with those memories?
- Are there other possibilities for memory storage?
- Why, if human beings encode everything, is recall only fractional unless specific stimulation occurs?
- What enables some people (such as the patient, known as "S," of Soviet psychologist A.R. Luria who devised methods of forgetting and recalling images) to remember almost everything?
- What are images?
- How are images stored and recalled?
- What enables the brain to transform the written word (two-dimensional) into vivid images in three-dimensional form?

Stanford University neurophysiologist Karl Pibram and others postulated possible answers to these and other questions by drawing upon the analogy of the brain to a hologram. Holographic (Greek "holos" meaning "whole") photography was first produced in 1963 by inventor Dennis Gabor, who conceived the concept in 1947 and won a Nobel prize for his discovery in 1971.

A holographic photograph consists of a two-dimensional plate, interlaced with colliding light wave interference patterns. This plate is initially produced by shooting a laser light beam into a prism. This process splits the beam, half of which is aimed, via a reflecting mirror, directly at the photographic plate. The other half is reflected off another mirror to hit the object being photographed. Light waves then bounce off the object and hit the plate (Figure 9.1). The image is reconstructed by the light, a laser beam directed (at the same angle as the original laser beam) at the photographed place which at this point contains the light wave patterns. Created in space, in three-dimensional imagery, is the two-dimensional holographic photograph; but, regardless of the viewing angle, the three-dimensional image remains.

The astounding aspect of holography is that, if a fragment of the original plate is broken off, the fragment itself, when shot with the laser, recreates the whole image (though it will be fuzzier).

Also, the same holographic plate can store many different images if the laser strikes it at different angles each time. One cubic centimeter of the plate can store 10 billion pieces of information.

Brain/Holograph Similarities

The reason for the analogy between holographic photography and the brain is that the two perform similarly:
- Both form and create images
- Information is spread throughout the holograph as with the brain and both store information redundantly. This means that, even though certain types of information

FIGURE 9.1 – **Holographic Photograph**

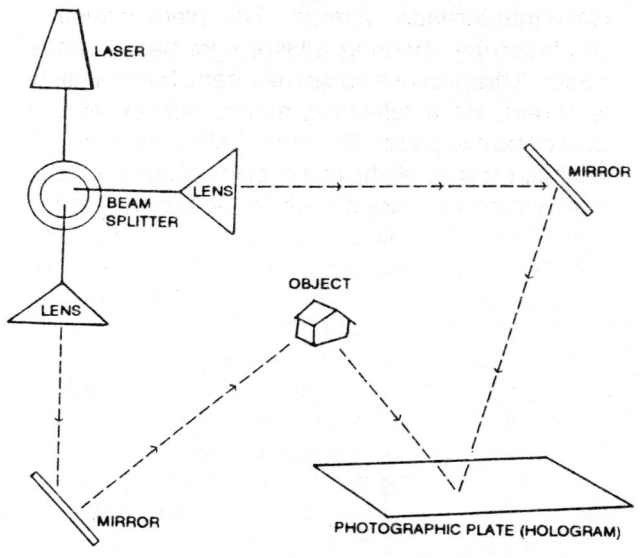

are stored in specific areas of the brain or hologram, those are not the only areas of storage
- A fragment of a shattered holographic photograph can recreate the whole, original image; similarly, after damage to the brain has occurred, those areas left intact have the potential to assume functions originally performed by the damaged areas
- Images formed by fragments of a shattered holograph or damaged brain are fuzzy; this phenomenon, which some researchers term interferences theory, may account for the "fuzzy recollections" which some people experience.

All things being equal (the absence of physiological brain damage and for pathological processors—such as senility or Alzheimer's disease), the common experience of forgetting (interference) occurs:

- When memories interfere with one another
- When new information blocks out old memories
- When old memories block out new information
- During states of hyperactivity, anxiety, and stress; at these times, the beta brain wave pattern (see Section #8) is so rapid that it acts like static on an AM radio. Thus, the message cannot get through
- The hologram currently is the only system, besides the brain, which has such a huge capacity for storage

Information Distribution and Processing: Two Models
The Neuroanatomical Brain Model

The brain distributes information through its neuroanatomical network, which contains 100 billion *neurons* (nerve cells) (Figure 9.2). These neurons serve as the building blocks of the brain. Each has at least 1,000 synaptic connections; and it is across these synapses, microscopic gaps between two adjacent neurons, that information is transmitted (Figure 9.3).

Transmitted information is called a *nerve impulse*. A nerve impulse moves from the neuron's cell body through the *axon*, a long fiber extending from the cell body of a neuron (Figure 9.3) to the synaptic button, at the terminal end of an axon. Here the nerve impulse is converted into *synaptic transmission*.

FIGURE 9.2 – A Typical Nerve Cell

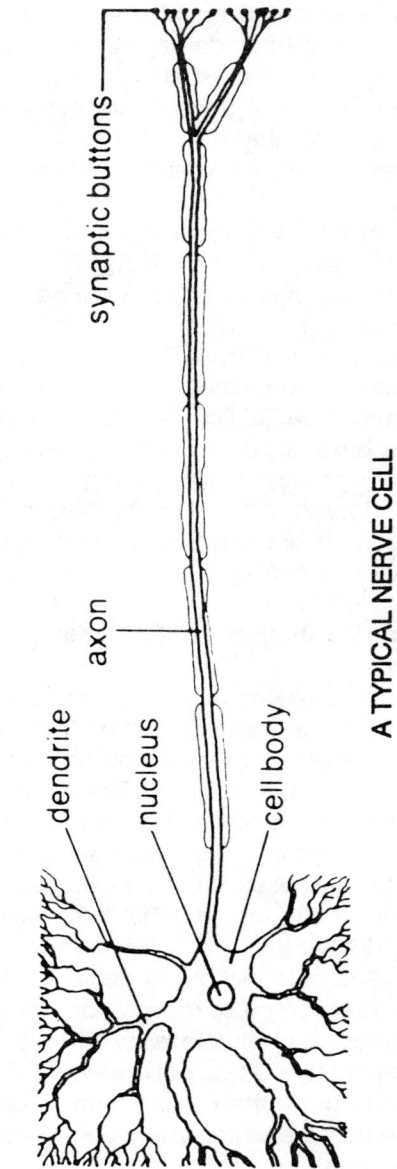

A TYPICAL NERVE CELL
(NEURON)

THE AMAZING BRAIN by Robert Ornstein and Richard Thompson, illustrated by David Macaulay. Illustrations copyright (c) 1984 by David A. Macaulay. Reprinted by permission of Houghton Mifflin Company. All rights reserved.

Synaptic Transmission

At this stage of transmission (Figure 9.4), information travels from the sending neuron to the *dendrite* of a receiving neuron (Figure 9.2). A dendrite is a short, fine branch extending from the cell body of the receiving neuron to the neighboring sending neuron across the synaptic gap. Information moves across synaptic gaps via chemical *neurotransmitter molecules*, after the electrical intensity has built up significantly enough to trigger the transmission (Figure 9.4).

The Holographic Brain/Mind Interactive Model
Holographic Patterning

Pribram's early research helped pioneer the creation of the neuroanatomical model of information distribution described above, and the researcher believes that this model is accurate. However, he also believed that information is distributed, processed, stored, and retrieved by other means as well.

Pribram believed that memories are encoded within chemical *patterns*, which are created through the wave action of neuronal dendrites (similar to wave patterns formed by a breeze moving through a wheat field). The dendrite waves move through *neuroglia* ("nerve glue"), special cells surrounding each neuron to provide them with nourishment and support. The waves interact with the waves of other dendrites to form the chemical patterns.

The fact that neuroglia increase in number as learning and experience increase and are enriched, lends further support to the holographic brain/mind interactive model. It is interesting to note, for example, that Einstein's brain (his cortex

FIGURE 9.3 – **Detail of a Synapse**

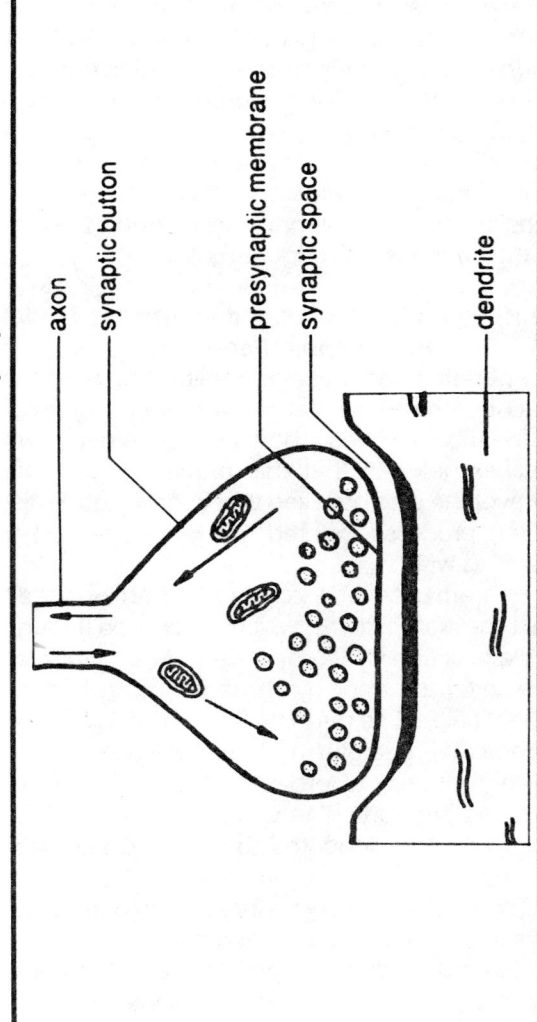

THE AMAZING BRAIN by Robert Ornstein and Richard Thompson, illustrated by David Macaulay. Illustrations copyright (c) 1984 by David A. Macaulay. Reprinted by permission of Houghton Mifflin Company. All rights reserved.

was preserved) contains 73 percent more neuroglia in a certain portion of the left hemisphere than others to which it has been compared.

Patterning Sequence

Information is relayed according to a patterned sequence. When a person sees an object or event, the information is conveyed to a set of neurons, which react by relaying the information to a second set of neurons. The relay of information occurs in two ways:

- By synaptic transmission via the neuroanatomical brain system
- By radiation of slow wave action via holographic processing

Pribram hypothesized that this second set of neurons analyzes the input and sends the results to a third set of neurons, which build the patterning of molecules that comprises the three-dimensional holographic image of the object or event seen. Pribram's research also indicates that these images seem to be imprinted as memories not inside the neurons but at and around the synapses of the neurons.

Thus, images reside in the brain (as on a holographic photographic plate) by the creation of wave actions (a holograph's light waves) and patterning. This process allows human beings to convert the written word (two-dimensional) into vivid images in three-dimensional form; ie, it allows for *imagination*:

IMAGe IN AcTION
or
wave action

FIGURE 9.4 – Synaptic Transmission

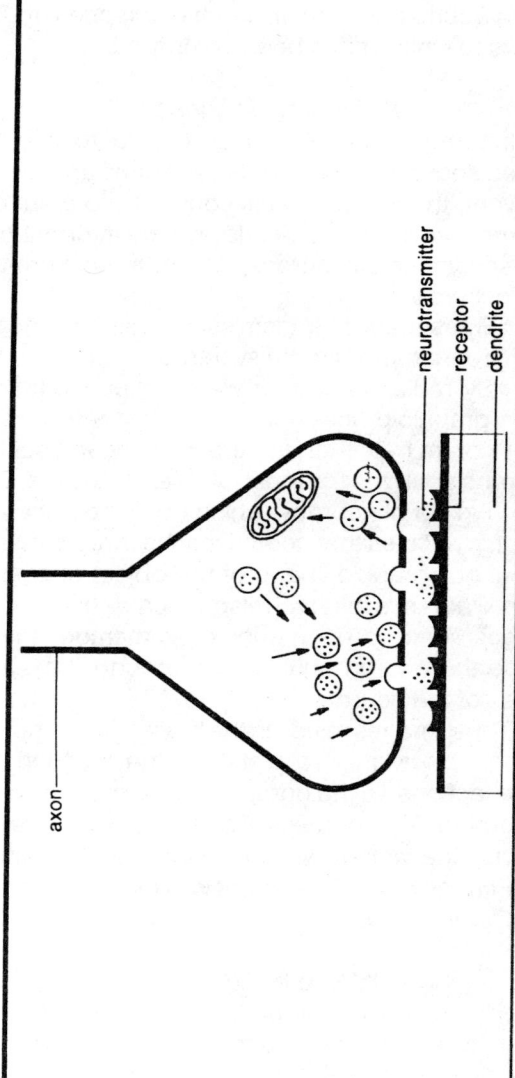

THE AMAZING BRAIN by Robert Ornstein and Richard Thompson, illustrated by David Macaulay. Illustrations copyright (c) 1984 by David A. Macaulay. Reprinted by permission of Houghton Mifflin Company. All rights reserved.

General Implications of the Holographic Brain

Because the brain can form "holographic" images and patterns, it stands to reason that human beings have the capability of:

- Association
- Behavior Patterning
- Recognition

Additionally, because the brain can generate whole pictures, perceptions, and/or recognitions from fragments of an imprinted pattern or stored image, it stands to reason that:

- A word can trigger the memory of a poem
- A song can trigger memories of past experiences associated with it, which, in turn, can trigger other associations, which trigger others, etc.
- An aroma can call forth memories of past events; for example, the smell of burning leaves may remind one of childhood autumn experiences, such as football games, a harvest moon, etc.
- An event can automatically stimulate a set of learned, conditioned responses; for example, a military man may react to an exploding firecracker by diving into a foxhole

Specific Implications of the Holographic Brain
Background: Space and Time

The holographic photograph and the holographic brain both contain vast storage spaces; but another component, the space between physical objects, is also important in comparing the two. Both entities transcend their physicality. A holographic photograph creates a three-dimensional image outside the boundaries of a two-dimensional, physical solid (the plate). The holographic brain works the same way. As a person reads information from a flat surface, the mind creates pictures or images from that information.

Transcending Space

The holograph represents the ability of objects to interact with each other by transcending space. The holographic model of the brain illustrates the same principle, ie, interactions among people which transcend space. For example, a person can telephone a lover who is 200 miles away and feel the physical and emotional sensations of hugging and touching. The sensations are real, and, in the caller's mind, the two are actually together. Even if the lovers part ways, the memories of such sensations can be recalled.

Another example of interaction is from the field of *psychoneuroimmunology* (the interaction of mind, body and the immune system): the thought of a stressor can trigger both emotional and physiological reactions, even when the stressor is no longer present (see Section #6).

Still another example is from the field of neuro-linguistic programming: as two people feel comfortable with each other and in "synch" with each other, they tend to display similar non-verbal language.

A final example is from the seemingly disparate fields of music and physics (non-linear dynamics): sound vibrations (music) produce recurring physiological patterns (physics) which can be measured by such equipment as the computer and macroscope.

Transcending Time

The holographic model also helps illustrate interactions which transcend time. The phantom pain of an amputated body part is an example of this, as are dreaming, daydreaming, and songs which conjure vivid memories. In each instance, a person senses being in two places at once: his physical location and his mental and/or emotional location. The conjured memories and images, their vividness, and the emotions associated with them are real.

Additional Implications

A physiological, philosophical, and spiritual question arises: Is the mind apart from the brain or a part of it? Regardless of the answer, a person — through his brain, frontal lobes, cortex, limbic system, left and right hemispheres, etc. — is able not only to react to and act upon stimuli but also is able to have aspirations, create goals, and make and initiate plans. The abilities of thought and emotion and the concomitant physiological acts make the human species unique, and it is the cortex (the most recent evolution of the brain) that assists in these abilities.

The mind, that wave-patterning stream of consciousness, interacts with the physical brain. The dual bodies — the brain/mind and the body — relate to and with each other to unify the human being, hence the view of the holographic brain model as the holographic brain/mind interactive model.

Healthcare Implications

As stated, the brain and body interact with each other. Messages are sent from the body to the brain and vice versa, and mental images (stimuli) can call forth physical sensations (responses). Additionally, researchers have found that specific types of stimuli can call forth specific types of responses; for example, the stimuli of images, Baroque music, relaxation and breathing techniques, etc. can actually elicit the response of accelerating the healing process (see Section #3). It stands to reason, then, that human beings, because of the interaction between their brains and bodies, can aid their own healing processes by creating the specific mental images that call forth the response of healing.

Many medical studies have investigated the use and advantage of mental imagery in the treatment of disease and have indicated that patients actually become "co-therapists" with their physicians by subscribing to a strong belief system and by becoming psychologically hardy and willing to implement activities which integrate the body and brain.

It is important that individuals first learn about the disease in question (ie, its patterns and symptoms, etc.) and then learn about the prescribed medical therapy, including drugs (ie, how they treat and/or manage the illness, side effects which may occur). *Acceptance* of the facts of a disease does not mean *abnegation* to its consequences. Once these left-brained activities are completed (learning), patients can then implement right-brained activities (imaging and patterning) to supplement and assist prescribed medical treatment. What is advocated is not disregard for illness and medical treatment but instead true representation of holistic health, ie, a left-brained approach (traditional medicine) supplemented by a right-brained approach — (the integration of accelerated learning and healing methods such as imagery, music therapy, relaxation techniques, and affirmations (see Sections #11, 13, 15, 16). As Lozanov discovered, learning and health are integrated (see Section #3). Therefore, patients should be taught accelerated learning skills not only to accelerate their learning but also to more efficiently implement prescribed medical treatment and to accelerate the entire healing process.

Patients should neither expect nor desire doctors to take full responsibility for their healing. Such an attitude is costly to both patients and physicians. Given rising health care costs and the current trend toward home health care, patients can no longer afford the "Doc, here I am; cure me" attitude. Additionally, without involving patients in their own care, physicians cannot be assured that their orders will be correctly executed. Through patient involvement in their own care and their use of integrated left- and right-brain approaches to health care, physicians may be better assured that patients are taking their medications and performing prescribed therapies as directed. Thus patients are more likely to accelerate their own healing.

Educational Implications

The interaction of the brain and body and of the left and right cerebral hemispheres has enormous educational implications. Mental imagery has been used traditionally as a mnemonic device for centuries, but its use also aids in accelerating the learning process. Luria's famous patient "S," for example, worked almost exclusively with imagery.

It is important that educators remember that values, belief systems, and expectations become especially important during the teaching of mental imagery, because of the holographic brain's transcendence of time and space when it is engaged in imaging. Therefore, a self-fulfilling prophecy, positive or negative, is likely to occur with students. If an educator and/or student believes he/she can learn, he/she will; if the educator and/or student does not believe he/she can learn, he/she won't. Expectations, especially those gained from imaging the outcome of the learning process, are extremely important.

This approach is similar to the placebo effect sometimes used in health care. Studies prove the power of this effect and conclude that the best indicator of health, in spite of objective laboratory tests and sophisticated instrumentation and technology, is still the subjective attitude of the patient regarding his/her own health status.

People create imagery associated with their beliefs about a situation, whether is applies to health care or to learning, and those images (fragments of the hologram) are encoded upon the brain as memory patterns which can be recalled for any purpose, positive or negative.

This author believes that educators should instruct students in the use of imagery to create a desired result. He believes that students already know the material under study and that his task is to help them, through teaching imagery skills, to recall and apply that information.

Sections #21 through 27 explain in detail the application of accelerated learning techniques to both training and education.

References: 1, 13 17, 19, 22, 24, 34

NOTES

#10 Brain Dominance and Learning Styles: An Overview

Specific tools for accelerated learning (see Sections #11 through #16) have been developed based upon brain/mind research findings. Especially significant to the development of these accelerated learning techniques was *lateralization:* the specialized cognitive functions of the left and right cerebral hemispheres (see Section #7).

As noted previously, the human brain has two cerebral hemispheres and two portions representing the limbic systems. Much of the human anatomy and physiology can be likened to a duplex "house," in that man has two (left and right) arms, legs, feet, eyes, and hands.

For movement and position, during early childhood, human beings manifest a *preference* or tendency toward the use of one side of their bodies over the other. This preference is termed *dominance*. Examples of dominance include:
- Reaching out with one hand, arm, foot, and/or leg
- Seeing — Having one eye dominant over the other in terms of first focusing upon a visual field and then physically seeing the object(s) in that field

Reasons for Dominance

There are three basic reasons for dominance. These are:
- Society and culture
- Survival
- Physical effectiveness and efficiency

Society and Culture

A child may have had natural preferences for using one or the other hand. Today, however, most people are right-handed. Why? Over the centuries of Western-Judeo civilization, natural left-handers were stigmatized; it was "wrong" to be left-handed. Only in the last few decades has this cultural taboo begun to be lifted. Consequently, left-handedness is on the increase.

Survival

Natural dominance preferences arise because of the brain's chief function to aid the body in survival. Ned Herrmann, President of the Brain Dominance Institute (see Section #35), believes that dominance gives the individual an automatic lead response to any situation. Herrmann indicates that dominance enhances one's ability to respond both efficiently and quickly be eliminating a decision step (Ref 25). For example, "What foot and leg and arm shall I start off with in order to get out of here?" One doesn't' have to think in this sequence before reacting; one automatically reacts.

Physical Effectiveness and Efficiency

Herrmann also believes that dominance enables the person to hone his/her physical skills. Repetition and practice lead to effective and efficient gross and fine motor coordination and strength. This occurs well beyond what would happen if a physical appendage (arm, hand, leg, foot) were utilized only half as much.

Cognitive Brain Dominance

A person prefers parts of the physical body over the other. This is what is meant by dominance. A person has preferences as well in how he\she prefers to understand, to learn, to express (both verbally and non-verbally), to think, etc. These are termed *cognitive preferences*. This is what is meant by

brain dominance.

Cognitive preferences are the ones used for solving problems, learning, processing stimuli and information, etc. Examples are:

- Do we buy a car based on our "gut level feel" for the car? Its styling, color, shape? (Right hemisphere preference, see Section #7.) Do we buy the car because of its specifications? Weight; steering radius; estimated miles per gallon, etc. These are left hemispheric preferences (see Section #7)
- What were my best school subjects? To what teachers and their teaching methods did I respond to the best? With what study methods did I learn and remember more?
- What profession(s) have I chosen for a career? (There is a direct relationship between occupational profile, cognitive and learning preferences)

From one's cognitive preferences, one easily develops one or more preferred modes of thinking and learning styles. These can be measured. If one is aware of *how* we think and learn, he/she can adopt learning methods that naturally fit, match his/her natural learning style(s). Knowing this has tremendous ramifications for not only learning but also daily communication, career development, work productivity, etc.

The Herrmann Brain Dominance Instrument

Several instruments have been devised to determine brain dominance and to assess cognitive processing and learning styles. The author recommends the Herrmann Brain Dominance Instrument (HBDI) for the following reasons:

- It has been researched thoroughly by independent professionals and organizations, including Princeton University's Educational Testing Service
- It has been assessed to be reliable and valid
- It closely approximates the Myers-Briggs Type Indicator, a popular psychological assessment tool
- It accounts for limbic system functions regarding emotions, information processing, learning, and memory (see Section #6)
- It has gained wide usage (more than 500,000 assessments through 1988)

The Four-Quadrant Model

Herrmann integrated the functions associated with the right and left cerebral hemispheres and right and left halves of the limbic system to create a quadratic model of thinking and learning (see Figures 10.1 and 10.2). Each quadrant indicates a different information processing mode (Ref 25). These four quadrants are described as follows, reading counterclockwise: (Descriptions derive from the HBDI. See Ref 25 and Table 10.1: *Brain Dominance: Definition of Terms.*)

- *Upper Left Cerebral* (Quadrant *A*, Figure 10.2) Key descriptors for an *Upper Left thinker* are:
  - Logical

FIGURE 10.1 – The Interconnected Brain System Quadratic Model

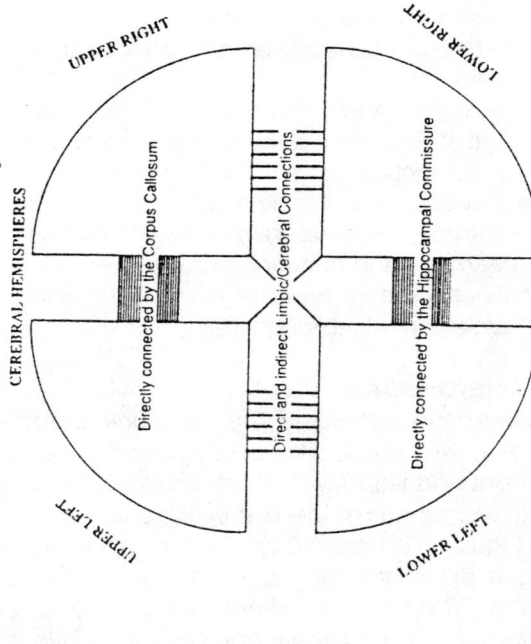

Herrmann N: The Creative Brain. Lake Lure, NC: Brain Books, 1988. Reprinted with permission by the Ned Herrmann Group, Applied Creative Services, Ltd.

- Analytical
- Mathematical
- Technical
- Problem solving
- Quantitative

General profile statement: This person thinks in words and numbers.

Overall profile descriptor: *Facts*.

- *Lower Left Limbic* (Quadrant *B*, Figure 10.2) Key descriptors for a *Lower Left* thinker are:
  - Controlled
  - Conservative
  - Planning
  - Organized
  - Administrative
  - Sequential
  - Procedural

General profile statement: This person thinks in words and/or "rules."

Overall profile descriptor: *Form*.

- *Lower Right Limbic* (Quadrant *C*, Figure 10.2) Key descriptors for a *Lower Right* thinker are:
  - Interpersonal
  - Emotional
  - Musical
  - Spiritual

General profile statement: This senses, "thinks" in feeling.

Overall profile descriptor: *Feelings*.

- *Upper Right Cerebral* (Quadrant D, Figure 10.2) Key discriptors for an Upper Right thinker are:
  - Visual
  - Creative
  - Synthesizer

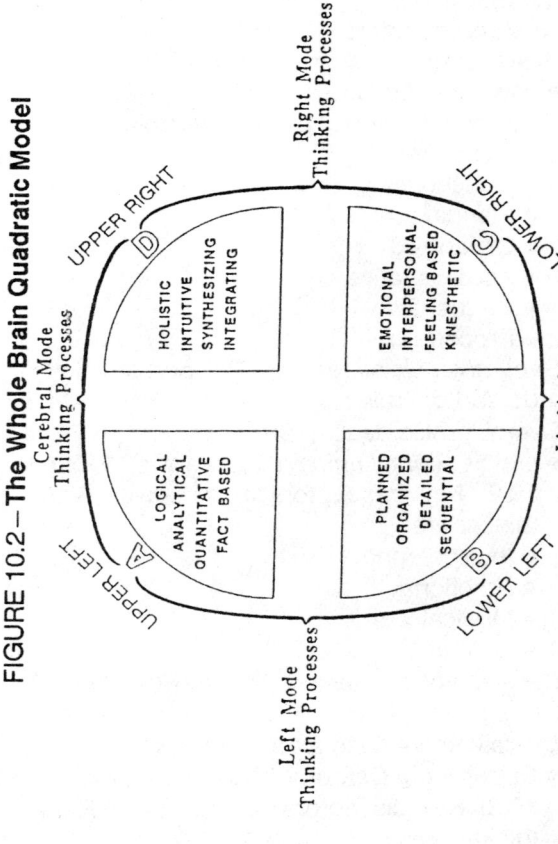

FIGURE 10.2 – The Whole Brain Quadratic Model

Herrmann N: The Creative Brain. Lake Lure, NC: Brain Books, 1988. Reprinted with permission by the Ned Herrmann Group, Applied Creative Services, Ltd.

- Artistic
- Holistic
- Conceptual
- Risk-taker
- Entrepreneur
- Simultaneous

General profile statement: This person thinks in images (see Section #11).

Overall profile descriptor: *Fantasy.*

Assessment

For assessment purposes, the four quadrants are subdivided into three descriptive components, each of which is assigned a number range (1 to 3) on a continuum of 0 to 100 (Table 10.1 and Figure 10.3). Descriptions of the quadrant numerical assessments are:

No.	Descriptor	Statement/Definition	Assessment/Score Range
1	Dominant	I *prefer* using this mode of cognitive processing.	67-100
2	Use	I recognize the *necessity* for using this mode.	34-66
3	Avoidance	I will not use this mode of processing. I *avoid* it.	0-33

The HBDI should be administered by a trained, certified professional. The raw score of each quadrant, based on answers from the assessment instrument, is converted into a descriptor number (see above) for each quadrant; these numbers made up a four-number descriptor profile (see example below). Subjects are then pro-

FIGURE 10.3 – **Herrmann Brain Dominance Profile**

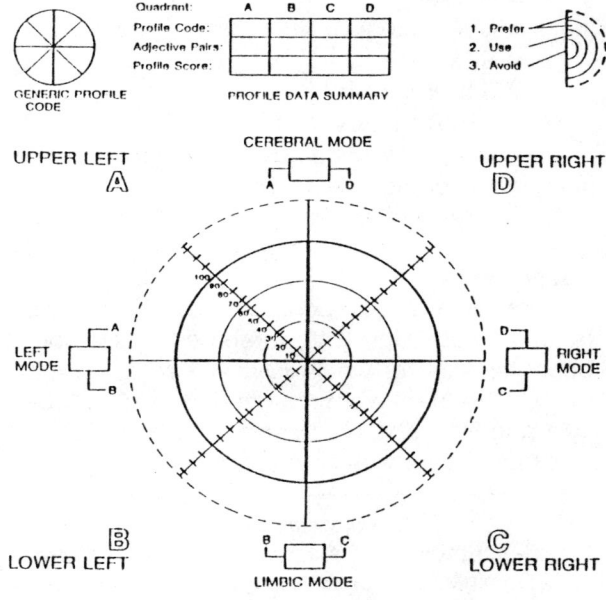

Reprinted with permission by the Ned Herrmann Group, Applied Creative Services, Ltd., 1986.

vided with narrative explanations of each descriptive number and an overall brain dominance profile assessment.

Figure 10.4 illustrates the HBDI profile of general practitioners, ie, 1-2-1-1 (see Appendix B for narrative description). Because the probability that all general practitioners will have similar profiles is high, a composite occupational profile can be made by averaging the mean scores of all assessed general practitioners (one descriptor number per quadrant); a graphic picture of the score within each quadrant can then be drawn.

Representative listings of other health care professionals' profiles and their narrative descriptions are provided in Appendices A and B, respectively.

Additional Assessment Information

A few generalizations can be made regarding individual assessment:

- Value judgments are not reflected in final scores; each quadrant type has situational advantages
- Strong correlations between the personal and learning profiles are apparent (see below, Learning Styles), with correspondingly strong correlations between learning and occupational profiles
- In the U.S., quadrant dominance rates are approximately:
  - For single dominance (preferring one quadrant only) — 30 percent
  - For multi-dominance (preferring two or more quadrants):
    - Double dominance — 40 percent
    - Triple dominance — 25 percent
    - Quadruple (no) dominance — 5 percent
- Approximately 70 percent of cognitive preferences are derived from environmental factors and 30 percent are innate, meaning that individuals can draw from non-dominant quadrants to aid learning

Illustrative Application
Interrelationships

Communication is vital to the strengthening and maintenance of interpersonal relationships. The HBDI can enhance communication by identi-

FIGURE 10.4 – **Example of Dominance Occupational Profile**

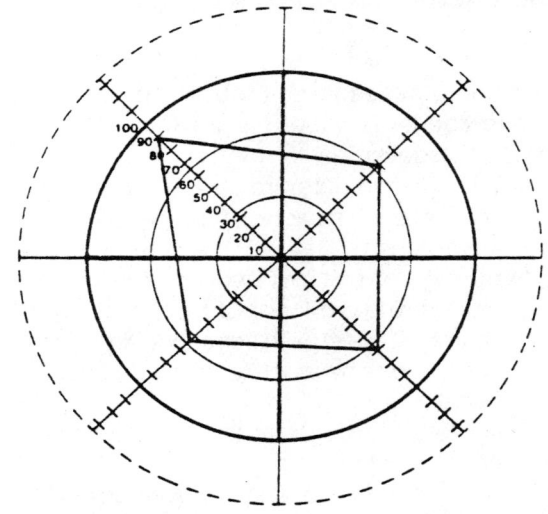

GENERAL PRACTITIONER - 1-2-1-1

Herrmann N: The Creative Brain. Lake Lure, NC: Brain Books, 1988. Reprinted with permission by the Ned Herrmann Group, Applied Creative Services, Ltd.

fying dominant modes of thinking so that individuals may better understand others' thinking processes and respond accordingly.

Occupational Relationships

In the same way that the HBDI can be used to enhance interpersonal relationships it can be used to help co-workers understand each other and deal effectively with occupational situations. One example of increased understanding involves the HBDI profile of school administrators in the U.S. Ninety-five percent of the school administrators assessed are lower-left dominant, indicating their tendency to ponder rather than implement school system reforms. School personnel, parents, students, and communities may better understand why school systems changes occur so slowly when they understand the mode of thinking of most school administrators.

Learning Styles and the HBDI

There is a strong correlation between a person's general cognitive profile and their preferred learning style(s). These relationships are depicted in Figure 10.5 and Table 10.2. Generally, upper- and lower-left dominant learners need structure, safety, and security to be incorporated into their learning processes, even experiential ones. By contrast, lower- and upper-right dominant learners are experiential, preferring to learn skills by performing them, by doing. In this book, Sections #1 through #16 have been written with the Upper- and Lower-Left learners in mind. They need the scientific base, the evaluation results, before attempting something new. On the other hand, the Upper- and Lower-Right learners may wish to begin this book with Sections #17 through #20, referring to any previous sections for reference as needed.

By identifying their own learning styles, adopting similarly-styled learning methods, and combining these factors with accelerated learning methods and study aids (see Sections #11 through #16), individuals can greatly enhance their learning (see Section #4).

Resources: See Section #35, No. 2 and No. 3

References: 9, 25, 26

FIGURE 10.5 — Herrmann Whole Brain Teaching and Learning Model

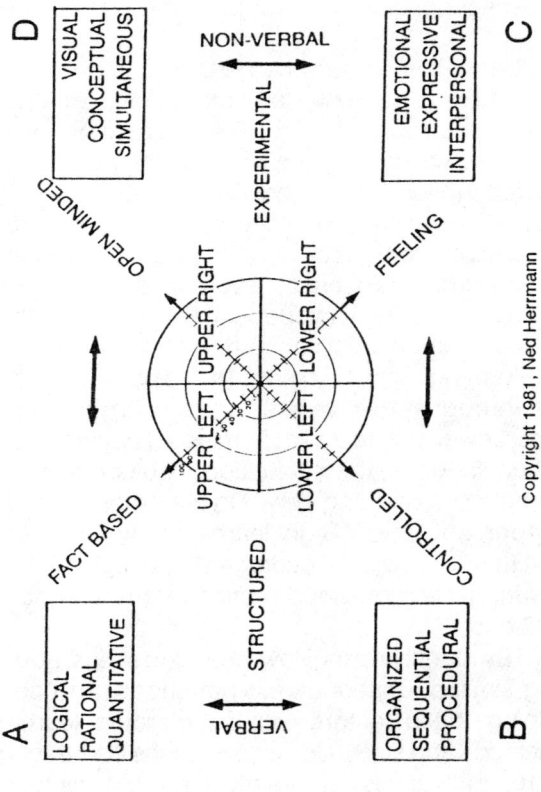

Bowser JM: Basic Dominance, Quadrantic Information Processing: A Brain Related Model. Columbus, OH: Vimach Associates, 1988, pg. 64.

TABLE 10.1 – **Brain Dominance: Definition of Terms**

The following terms include, but are not limited to, those listed within the sub-section, the Herrmann Brain Dominance Instrument, the four quadrants, as illustrated in Figure 8.2.

Analytic: Breaking up things or ideas into parts and examining them to see how they fit together.

Artistic: Taking enjoyment from or skillful in painting, drawing, music, or sculpture. Able to coordinate color, design, and texture for pleasant effects.

Conceptual: Able to conceive thoughts and ideas—to generalize abstract ideas from specific instances.

Controlled: Restrained, holding back, in charge of one's emotions.

Conservative: Tending toward maintaining traditional and proven views, conditions, and institutions.

Creative: Having unusual ideas and innovative thoughts. Able to put things together in new and imaginative ways.

Emotional: Having feelings that are easily stirred; displaying those feelings.

Holistic: Able to perceive and understand the "big picture" without dwelling on individual elements of an idea, concepts, or situation. Can see the forest as contrasted with the trees.

Interpersonal: Able easily to develop and maintain meaningful and pleasant relationships with many different kinds of people.

Logical: Able to reason deductively from what has gone before.

Mathematical: Perceiving and understanding numbers and being able to manipulate them to a desired end.

Musical: Having an interest in or talent for music and/or dance.

Organized: Able to arrange people, concepts, objects, elements, etc. into coherent relationships with each other.

Planning: Formulating methods or means to achieve a desired end in advance of taking actions to implement.

Problem solving: Able to find solutions to difficult problems by reasoning.

Quantitative: Oreinted toward numerical relationships, inclined to know or seek exact measures.

Sequential: Dealing with things and ideas one after another or in order.

Simultaneous: Able to process more than one type of mental input at a time, eg, visual, verbal, and musical. Able to attend to more than one activity at a time.

Spiritual: Having to do with spirit or soul as apart from the body or other material things.

Synthesizer: One who unites separate ideas, elements or concepts into something new.

Technical: Able to understand and apply engineering and scientifc knowledge.

Modified from Bowser JM: Basic Dominance, Quadrantic Information Processing: A Brain Related Model. Columbus, OH: Vimach Associates, 1988, Pg. 8-9.

TABLE 10.2 — Learning Styles Represented by the Specialized Modes of the Four Quadrants

A — Upper Left	D — Upper Right
LEARNS BY:	**LEARNS BY:**
Acquiring and quantifying facts Applying analysis and logic Thinking through ideas Building cases Forming theories	Taking initiative Exploring hidden possibilities Relying on intuition Self discovery Constructing concepts Synthesizing content
B — Lower Left	C — Lower Right
LEARNS BY:	**LEARNS BY:**
Organizing and structuring content Sequencing content Evaluating skills through practice Implementing course content	Listening and sharing ideas Integrating experiences with self Moving and feeling Harmonizing with the content Emotional involvement Copyright, Ned Herrmann 1986

Bowser JM: Basic Dominance, Quadrantic Information Processing: A Brain Related Model. Columbus, OH: Vimach Associates, 1988, Pg. 68.

#11 Imagery

Definition
Imagery is the art of producing images. Thus, mental imagery is the art of producing mental images as a natural outcome of the imagination.

Characteristics
Sensory Integration
Imagery should not be confused with visualization. Such an approach excludes the 40 percent of the population which, according to Remen, can feel and hear images but cannot visualize them (Ref 37). Human beings actually have six, rather than five, senses, all of which should be utilized to enhance imagery and learning:
- Vision
- Hearing
- Touch
- Taste
- Smell
- Motion

True imagery employs all of the senses. The greater the number of senses employed by the imagination, the truer and more effective the imagery. In like manner, the greater the number of senses employed during the imaging step of the learning process, the more effective and efficient the learning.

Multi-Level Sensory Integration
The six senses can be used on all four consciousness levels:
- Conscious physical level
- Conscious mental (imaginative) level

- Paraconscious level (see Section #2)
- Subconscious level — At this level, senses and images reveal themselves primarily through dreams, though other applications exist. Siegel, for example, found that anesthetized patients hear and understand his orders and respond physiologically to his requests (Ref 40); comatose patients also hear the sounds of their environments

Application to Learning and Memory — Mnemonics

Although human beings think in images, they often are only paraconsciously aware of doing so. For example, at the verbalization of the name of a favorite football team, a person mentally creates visual images and conjures feelings associated with the team rather than creating images of the actual words used to describe the team.

Perhaps imagery was man's first method of thinking (early Grecians worshipped Mnemosyne, the goddess of memory, from whom the term mnemonics is derived). Long before scientists knew of cerebral hemispheric specialization and developed the concept of the holographic brain, the Greeks developed the major principles of memory retention:

- Association — Linking new information with old
- Imagination — Using mental images to depict an association between new and old information

Principles of Active Imagination

As noted previously, the more creative the imagination and the greater the number of senses

employed in imaging, the greater the memory recall. This tenet has been confirmed time and again and became the basis for the development of the principles of active imagination. These principles have proven to be effective in enhancing memory when applied in conjunction with activation of the brain's natural functioning abilities and of the six senses. The principles of active imagination are:
- The more unrestricted the imagination, the greater the chance of memory retention; images are more likely to aid recall if they are:
  - Obscene
  - Nonsensical
  - Ridiculous
  - Absurd
  - Sexual
  - Sensual
  - Bizarre
- The more colors used in images, the better the retention
- The grander the scale of the image, the greater the chances of recall
- The more specific and familiar the details of the image, the better the chances of associating new and old information and, thus, memory retention and recall. Abstract images offer fewer means of associations; specific terms used to describe images should be grounded in familiarity and consist mainly of nouns (eg, shapes of letters, word lengths, etc.). Even pronunciations of terms should be imagined
- The greater the incorporation of the six senses in the image, the greater the chances

of recall because of the link of sensory integration with memory storage and retrieval via the limbic system (see Section #6). The powerful sense of smell, for example, can trigger many associations, as can the sense of motion
- Learning involves self-responsibility. No person can tell another how to create an image or what an image should consist of. Every person must create images that are effective for him/her
- Order and sequence (structural requirements for left-dominant individuals) are necessary if associations are to occur. Images of new information must relate to familiar (old) information and symbolize specific items if the new terms or concepts they depict are to be remembered and if confusion is to be avoided. Keeping images simple also helps to avoid memory interference (see Section #9)

Principles of Association

Principles of association that apply to traditional memory systems include:
- Using a key memory word as the associative link between new and old information
- Using order and sequencing techniques in imagery

Integrating Association and Imagination Principles

By integrating the principles of imagery and association, individuals can enhance memory storage and retrieval. An example of the integration of the two systems is illustrated in Table 11.1.

TABLE 11.1 – Evolutionary Development of the Major Components of the Triune Brain

The Format: Imagery Technique (image, description or picture)	New Information (Number representing sequential development)	Association (Component, definition, key words and phrases)
The Integration: Einstein rides a rainbow across a blue-skied universe, his left hand holding the rainbow's reins and his right inscribing $E=MC^2$ across the universe with an elongated pen. (The pen = the number 1.)	1. Human brain	This brain is the newest in human evolution. It contains the left and right hemispheres.
Two swans soar happily and effortlessly in the sky above two seahorses who are water-skiing. (The two swans, shaped like a "2" = the number 2 and the two halves of the limbic system. Happily = emotion. Effortless, water-skiing = physical function. Blue = men-	2. Mammalian brain	This brain is the second oldest in human evolution. It contains the limbic system.

tal authority and relaxation. Seahorses = mammals, and hippocampus of limbic system is of similar shape.)		
An alligator eats three watermelons stacked upon each other for breakfast while an alarm clock blares in the background. (Three melons = the number 3. The alarm = the alarm of the brain.)	3.	Reptilian brain	This brain is the oldest in human evolution. It contains the reticular activating system, the alarm bell of the brain.

The Explanation:

The numbers are the memory pegs created in the images. They simulate the shape of the item to be remembered, thus taking advantage of the number/shape mnemonic system (Ref 12).

The numbers also reinforce the sequence of brain evolution, thus becoming the key memory words for association and the peg which connects the image of the new information to the old. For association, the brain first recalls the image, picture, hieroglyph, symbol, logo, or parable and then uses the image to trigger recall.

Imagery Facilitates Recall

Ancient cultures used imagery (eg, hieroglyphics) to depict their histories and beliefs. Currently, some educators advocate a return to these "basics" to aid recall, based on the research that explains the phenomenon.

An interesting aspect of imagery is that it occurs in the right hemisphere of the brain, an area that does not recognize time. Though the events depicted through imagery may have occurred in the past, their associated images and descriptions and the recall of the events occur in the present. Thus, natural functions of the right hemisphere — (image creation and timelessness here the use of past and present) — are doubly reinforced.

Left/Right Note-Study System

The principles of imagination and association can be incorporated into a study system that even more effectively enhances learning and retention. An important point is the format in which study notes are written. Note-taking should be formatted to coincide with the processes of each cerebral hemisphere and the bodily functions that each hemisphere controls. Because the right hemisphere is the "artistic" side of the brain and because it controls the left side of the body, images used in note-taking should be drawn on the left side of the page. Accordingly, because the left hemisphere is the "language" side and controls the right side of the body, narrative descriptions and key terms (to be written in all capital letters) should be placed on the right side of the page. (This format was followed in the previous illustration [Table 11.1, also see, Figure 11.2] of the integration of association and imagination principles.)

Even vision plays a role in information processing. Though each eye sends its messages to the corresponding hemisphere of the brain, the information sent by one eye is processed by the opposite side of the brain (Figure 11.1).

(This text follows the left-right note-study system format of placing graphics on the left-hand page and narrative on the right so as to more closely assimilate the natural functions of the brain. [See Appendix C for specific format guidelines.])

Another example of the left/right note study system is illustrated in Figure 11.2, Examples 1, 2, 3 and 4.

In addition to using the left-right note-study system for note-taking, it is a excellent tool for the review of study notes and test preparation.

EXERCISE: Use the "Notes" pages found at the ends of various sections of this text to practice the left-right note-study system, remembering to incorporate as many of the principles of association and imagination as possible.

Mind-Mapping

The left/right study system can be supplemented by mind-mapping, a system developed by Buzan (Ref 12) which draws upon the right hemisphere (visuo-spatial imagery) and the holographic brain to cluster related information in a non-linear form.

Guidelines

Specific guidelines must be followed in the development of a mind-map if the result is to be effective (Figure 11.3):

FIGURE 11.1 — Book Format, Example for Left-Right Note-Study System

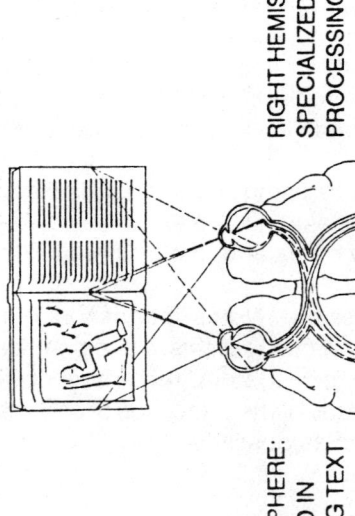

Modified from Herrmann N: The Creative Brain. Lake Lure, NC: Brain Books, 1988. Reprinted with permission by the Ned Herrmann Group, Applied Creative Services, Ltd.

- The central theme, whether it is a key term (capitalized) or an image, is to be placed at the center of the page
- Sub-themes (also capitalized) are to be placed in order of importance, with the most important item placed closest to the center and the least important placed at the outer edges of the mind-map
- Relationships among themes and sub-themes are to be indicated by connecting lines
- Closely-related concepts are to be clustered and each cluster color-coded
- Themes and sub-themes are to be indicated by key words or phrases; concepts can be indicated by images
- The mind-map must follow the principles of association and imagination

Advantages

One advantage of the mind-map is that it offers a view of the information that replicates the brain's ability to process bits of information simultaneously rather than in linear fashion. Buzan notes that human beings see printed matter in word clusters (the human being can fixate on as many as six words at once [Ref 11]), even though words are printed individually and linearly.

Another advantage of a mind-map is that it clearly indicates interrelationships among key words and concepts and the relative importance of each.

Additionally, review and recall are easier and less time-consuming with mind-mapping than with traditional study systems.

FIGURE 11.2 – **Left/Right Note-Study System**

EXAMPLE 1

HIPPOCAMPUS — A part of the limbic system used for learning and short-term memory.

(Be there with "Hippy." Talk to him. Ask him what courses he's taking. Feel his mouth as he opens his mouth to speak.)

EXAMPLE 2

PATO — Spanish for duck. In language training, the Spanish noun for duck (pato) might be easily associated with a duck laying on a potato. The potato subliminally associates with "pato," and the image of the duck resembles the "p" and "t" of the Spanish term's spelling.

(Hear daffy quacking as you step through the potato patch.)

EXAMPLE 3

LARGO — Classical music of a slow tempo ranging from 42 to 66 beats per minute. This music is conducive to producing the alpha brain wave state.

(Picture your favorite outdoors setting and hear the echo of the music as it reverberates through the scene.)

EXAMPLE 4

ALPHA — The band of brain waves ranging from 8 to 13 cycles per second which is associated with relaxed yet alert learning states.

(As you sink into the chair, feel the relaxation roll through your body and hear the calming music. As you read and comprehend the material in the book, put the book down and discuss it with Einstein.)

FIGURE 11.3 – Mind Map

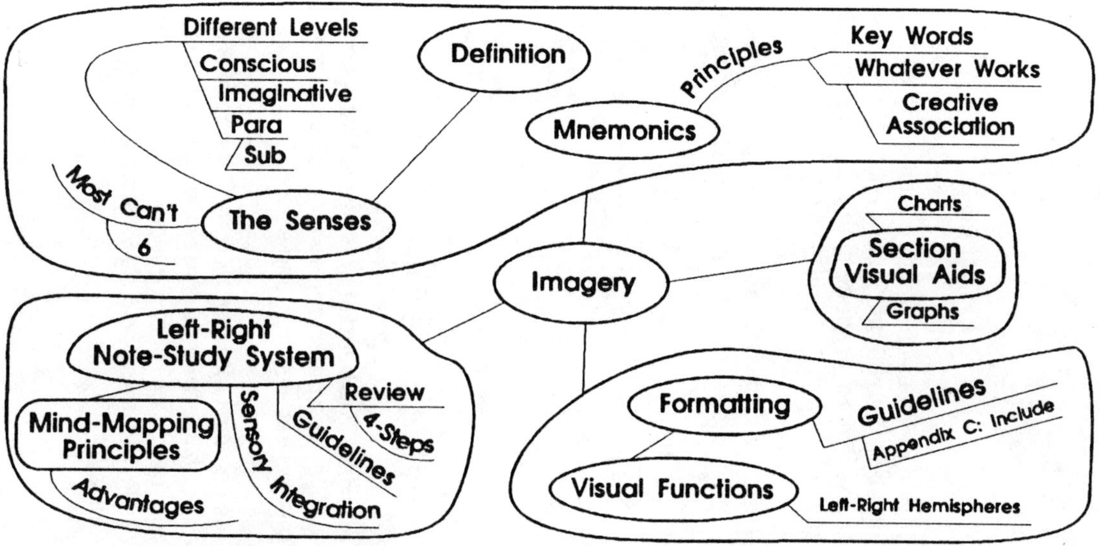

Integrating Mind-Mapping and Left/Right Note-Study Systems

Combining mind-mapping and the left/right note-study system increases the effectiveness of either device used singly. An additional benefit of the combination is that the learner is forced to become physically involved in the study process, another enhancement to learning.

References: 11, 12, 18, 25, 37, 40

#12 Peripheral Visual Aids

Definition
Peripherals are visual aids designed to facilitate:
- Creation and maintenance of a relaxed yet alert learning environment
- Initial learning
- Retention
- Memory recall

Characteristics
Within the context of learning, all visual aids can be classified as peripherals, including everything within the instructor's environment (even clothing colors and non-verbal communication). However, for the purposes of this text (ie, accelerated learning techniques applied specifically to the adult learner), peripheral visual aids are limited to:
- Printed matter (images and language) (see Section #35 for suggested readings and Resource #12 for instructional media)
- "Holographic extension" of notes and textual material; just as the three-dimensional image is an extension of the holographic plates, (see Section 9), a peripheral visual aid is an extension of study notes and texts
- Still-motion visual aids

Advantages/Disadvantages of Peripherals
Peripherals are advantageous to most styles of learning because they reinforce retention and recall. Combined with learning affirmations (see Section #13) and posters depicting a relaxation "sanctuary" (see Section #18), they also help to

develop and maintain a relaxed, positive learning environment. Additionally, by creating and using peripherals, students learn kinesthetically and take responsibility for their own learning.

Peripherals as still-motion visual aids are less advantageous for the teaching and learning of psychomotor skills and role modeling because they cannot display the motions required in the performance of such skills.

Construction Guidelines for Printed Material

One of the most common forms of communicating information is through printed matter (graphs, charts, posters, etc.); but for such materials to be effective, construction guidelines must be followed during their preparation and in their presentation.

Colors

Colors are especially important in the stimulation of the imagination (see Section #11) and should be used methodically in easel graphics. A text itself can be printed in colors that will aid retention and recall.

Different colors connote different psychological reactions. General psychological connotations associated with specific colors are:

- Blue—Mental authority; relaxation (especially dark blue); blue is also associated with slow musical movements (see Section #15). The use of blue along with appropriate music doubly reinforces the advantageous effects, and the two reinforce each other
- Red and orange—Physical energy; creativity; stimulation; also, red increases:
  - Appetite

- Blood pressure
- Heart rate
- Green — Healing; reduction of nervous and muscular tension; enhancement of a desire to act ("the green light")
- Yellow — Cheerfulness; stimulation
- Violet — Mystical; intuitive understanding
- Brown — Associations with the six senses; physical ease; sensuous contentment; familial security ("roots"); the hearth. Subliminally, browns and beiges convey a "trust me" message
- Peach and rose — Warmth; enhancement of spiritual will for physical healing

The best learning and counseling environments:

- Are decorated using a mixture of blue and earth tones (for relaxation)
- Have accents of reds and oranges (for creative stimulation)
- Offer natural lighting (see Section #17).

Lines and Columns

A correctly-formatted visual aid can stimulate learning. Whenever possible, information should be presented in two to three vertical columns that are divided by space rather than by vertical lines or bars. Vertical lines subliminally create barriers to information access and prevent the mind from seeing and making associations and relationships among the columns of information, whereas space divisions imply a transcendence of and associations and relationships among the information in each column. Pre-lined chart paper should never be used.

Wording and Symbols

Graphics developers should condense information as much as possible and adhere to such guidelines as:
- Using abbreviations wherever possible
- Using (capitalized) key words and phrases rather than long sentences
- Placing no more than five words on each line
- Making use of the principles of:
  - Left/right note-study system (see Section #11)
  - Imagination (see Section #11)
  - Mind-mapping (see Section #11)

Graphics developers also should remember that the larger the dimensions of the words or symbols written on easel graphics, the greater their visual impact on the viewer.

Guidelines for Using Peripherals in Self-Study

To make the best use of peripheral visual aids, learners should:
- Place peripherals in a physically-comfortable position, usually slightly above eye level (an angle greater than 45 degrees may cause neck tension)
- When mounting graphics on a wall, avoid cluttering the learning aid with thumb tacks or push pins; instead use an adhesive or other mounting material on the back side of the graphic
- Place graphics within peripheral vision
- When several graphics are used, arrange them in an organized fashion according to information they represent (eg, from general to specific or vice versa) and

according to the brain hemisphere function (see Section #7) required for effective learning (holistic, visuo-spatial, imagistic). A format sequence, for example, might include mind-map illustrations on the left and lists of specific terms and concepts on the right
- To avoid clutter in the study area, remove visual aids from view as the material pertaining to them is learned and retained. The only peripherals that should remain in view after material is learned include those that serve as:
  - Mind-maps
  - Building block reinforcers
  - Structure and order reinforcers

Special Considerations for Older Adult Learners

Additional guidelines must be considered when developing peripheral visual aids for older learners (see Section #27). These include:
- Color-coding — Because of age-related decreases in visual function, older learners often have difficulty distinguishing subtleties of color; therefore, graphics developers should use stronger and brighter color contrasts
- Placement of peripherals — With age, the range of vision (upward visual extension) diminishes; therefore, peripherals should be place at or near eye level
- Glare — One of the most common visual problems for older learners is cataracts, which can cause decreased tolerance to

glare; therefore, peripherals should be prepared on non-glossy surfaces and should be mounted and adjusted to avoid glare

References: 2, 6, 30, 43,

Resource: 12

#13 Learning Affirmations

Definitions and Characteristics

An *affirmation* is a positive, conscious statement of intent describing a specific event that has already been accomplished. Although this sounds like a contradiction, the implication of equating a statement of intent with a statement of completion is crucial to the effectiveness of an affirmation. To "affirm" means to "make firm"; but what is being made firm already exists, is already a reality that transcends time and space.

Thus, a *learning* affirmation is an explicit, positive, conscious statement of intent that makes firm the already existent learning. Much of learning, then, is a matter of recalling and using stored (thus existing) knowledge and skills. A learning affirmation is a tremendous motivational method for adult learners, since affirmations reinforce and maintain the motivation that adult learners generally possess. When they can positively answer the question "what's in it for me?" adult learners' self-motivation is enhanced, they recall what they want to remember, and learning takes place.

Advantages

Advantages of using learning affirmations are that:
- Learning affirmations foster self-motivation. An individual who develops affirmations for himself/herself is accepting the responsibility for his/her own learning
- Learning affirmations help create and maintain a relaxed yet alert learning environment

- Because of their uniqueness, learning affirmations add another dimension to study aids and help to create and fulfill the learner's expectations

Guidelines for the Development of Learning Affirmations

The following guidelines should be incorporated into the development of all learning affirmations (see Table 13.1 for examples):

1. Affirmations always begin with the words
   "I AM."

   This corresponds with the definition of an affirmation (ie, that the affirmation already exists) and with the idea of the adult taking responsibility for his own learning.

2. Affirmations contain present tense, positive wording.

The use of the present tense corresponds with right brain's realm of timelessness. Future tense is never used (eg, "I will learn" or "I will give up smoking") because such statements reinforce procrastination.

Positive wording is imperative if affirmations are to be effective. Negative wording and/or connotations undermine attempts at motivation and are not to be used in affirmations. How motivating, for example, are such statements as "I can't learn" and "I don't understand"? A learner can accept the reality of not understanding without embracing the negative connotation of such a statement by modifying the statement to say "Momentarily, I don't understand." This more positive statement implies an already existing intent to understand and the willingness to invest effort, time, and resources to acquire that understanding.

TABLE 13.1 – **Affirmations**

I AM RELAXED AND RECEPTIVE TO LEARNING THE MATERIAL PRESENTED TODAY.

I AM ABSORBING THE SKILLS AND KNOWLEDGE PRESENTED NOW.

I AM UTILIZING SKILLS AND KNOWLEDGE THAT FOSTER POSITIVE AND CONSTRUCTIVE GROWTH FOR THE GOOD OF ALL CONCERNED.

Copyright, R.G. Swartz and Associates 1990
MANAGEMENT IMPACT SKILLS

The *placebo* effect has been thoroughly documented in health care (see Section #14); its effect on patients' recovery has been strongly correlated with physicians' use of positive and negative language and non-verbal "messages." Which of the following approaches, for example, is more likely to result in the patient's recovery?

- "Look, this pill probably won't do you any good, and the side effects will not be pleasant, to say the least. But taking this medicine is probably better than not doing anything. Here are the instructions."
- "This drug has just been approved. The anticipated results are.... The side effects are.... Here are the instructions. My staff will help you monitor your improvement and any side effects you might experience while you take this drug. You know you are experiencing a serious disease, and you know the relevant facts. But you do not have to experience all the symptoms of the disease and all the side effects of the drug and probably will not do so. Now, what questions do you have?"

In like manner, the placebo effect is at work in the positive versus the negative wording of affirmations. The language used to express situations can make a tremendous difference in a person's ability to cope with whatever is at hand. A statement such as "I've got a problem" compounds the "problem" by increasing negativity. By contrast, a statement such as "I'm in a situation" implies the temporary nature of the ordeal and the expectation of getting through the difficult period.

However, even a seemingly positive statement may have its focus on a negative entity. The statement "I am free of stress," for example, seems to be positive, yet it focuses on the negative (stress) and implies that the stress still exists. A better, more positive, and correctly-focused statement would be "I am relaxed"; in this statement the focus is on the positive (relaxation) rather than the negative. Such a rhetorical innuendo is the reason that campaigns such as "Say No to Drugs" will not succeed. Saying "no" to something still focuses on the object being rejected. To be rid of one thing, another must take its place; and it is toward the replacement object that the focus should be directed (eg, "Say Yes to Relaxation").

3. The language used to state affirmations should be action-oriented. A word such as "absorbing" is such a word; it implies an effortless "soaking up" of the material being presented (much like a sponge, with which this word is subliminally associated).
4. Affirmations should be simply stated and contain only one implied goal, affirmed intent, or objective; a series of affirmations is to consist of a maximum of three statements.

The limited number of attempted goals implies the learner's tighter focus on those goals. If too many objectives are attempted at one time, the learner will falter. Because time and resources are often limited, learners are likely to accomplish goals more quickly and successfully if they set priorities and attempt no more than three goals at a time.

5. Affirmations must contain left-brain structure and logic.

Affirmations are most effective when they make logical sense to the learner. If the learner believes that the material to be learned is within the realm of reality as he/she perceives it and that he/she can acquire the skills and knowledge necessary for the attainment of his/her objectives, he/she can logically affirm that the learning will take place. Additionally, by his/her logical perception of the learning situation, he/she is taking the responsibility for his/her own learning; doing so logically implies the possibility of achieving desired learning goals.

6. Affirmations are most effective when they fit within the moral and ethical value systems of the learner.

    Learning affirmations must contain the ethical premises of:
    - Positive and constructive growth for the good of all concerned
    - The learner's own growth for greater effectiveness in business and personal situations

7. Affirmations should be stated in general, rather than specific, terms.

    Learning affirmations should be general enough to be applied to *any* learning situation.

Guidelines for the Use of Learning Affirmations

The following guidelines are recommended for the most effective utilization of learning affirmations:

1. Affirmations should be mounted on posterboard (recommended for permanency) or flip chart or easel graphic paper.
2. The guidelines for peripheral visual aids should be considered in the placement of affirmation posterboards within the study area.

3. Affirmation posterboards should take a prominent place in the study area so that the learner may be peripherally aware of them when he is not specifically focusing on them.
4. Affirmation posterboards should remain in the study area as "fixtures" throughout the study and learning processes, even though other peripheral reinforcers will be substituted along the way.
5. Images depicting stated affirmations, learning objectives, and achievements of objectives should be developed to coincide with affirmation posterboards. These depictions should follow the principles of association and imagination (see Section #11) and the sensory integration sequencing of relaxation exercises (see Section #18). They should be mounted on posterboard and positioned to the left of their corresponding affirmations (see Section #11, Left-Right Note-Study System). Alternatively, three-dimensional images of affirmations (eg, mobiles, sculptures) can be placed prominently in the study area.

References: 43

Resources: 15

NOTES

#14 Subliminals

Definition/Purpose

A subliminal is "any device or technique that is intentionally used to convey or attempts to convey a message to a person by means of images, writing, or sounds that are not consciously perceivable" (Ref 45). For the enhancement of learning, subliminals can:
- Aid in the creation and reinforcement of a relaxed yet alert learning environment
- Incorporate the subconscious senses into the learning process (see Section #2)

History

During the 1950s, a New Jersey theater owner encoded split-second visual advertisements (subliminals) into a film, showed the film to his audiences, and reported subsequent increased soda sales. Vance Packard described such applications of subliminals within the advertising industry in his 1957 book *The Hidden Persuaders*.

Throughout the late 1970s and early 1980s, department stores reported that their use of subliminals dramatically reduced shoplifting, and in 1980 a Missouri health care clinic documented reduced anxiety levels in patients who were subjected to subliminal stress management messages.

Lozanov was reported to have used *audio* subliminals in his early research. Though this report is unconfirmed, it is known that a key to Lozanov's foreign language training was his application of *visual* subliminals, similar to those used in the left-right note-study system example (see Section #11, Figure 11.2, Example 2) in which the "p" and "t" of pato (Spanish for duck) visually resemble the drawing of the duck.

Currently, the market for subliminal, self-help audiocassettes approximates a $50 million industry that continues to grow. Subliminal messages are being incorporated into videocassettes as well.

Characteristics

Learning can be enhanced when visual subliminals are embedded into imagery (see Example 2, Figure 11.2, Section 11) and lectures are accompanied by peripheral visual aids of learning affirmations (see Section #13). So utilized, visual subliminals become *supraliminals*, which are consciously unnoticed, visually. Once a sub- or supraliminal is recognized, it becomes a paraconscious peripheral.

Audio subliminals are embedded into musical selections and sound tracks, usually above and/or below the range of conscious sound frequency (human hearing).

Effectiveness

A plethora of research regarding the effectiveness of subliminal messages exists (Ref 45). Audio subliminal messages have been proven to be effective if they are appropriately done and ethically valid. Valid applications have occurred in the health care industry regarding the placebo effect of subliminal messages. A placebo (a Latin derivative meaning "I shall please") refers to an active or inactive treatment, therapy, or procedure that is integrated with a patient's belief system and produces a concomitant physiological healing effect. Because the placebo effect is tied to the belief system and because those things a person believes in are effective for that person, often it is the placebo that enhances healing, with the physiological activity produced by the treatment being irrelevant to the condition being treated. Research substantiates this theory (see Section #35, Resource 16; also Sec. 36, Reference 1).

Guidelines for Developing and Using Subliminals

All subliminals should be used appropriately and ethically. For effectiveness, certain guidelines should be followed in their development, regardless of the intended application.

Well-worded subliminals follow the guidelines for constructing affirmations (see Section #13), and effective visual subliminals follow the principles of association and imagination (see Section #11).

The use of subliminals and their message content need not be concealed from viewers/listeners in order for messages to be effective. Conscious awareness of subliminal messages does not detract from the impact of messages on the subconscious. In fact, knowing about the use of a subliminal message and knowing the message may enable a participant to incorporate the message, along with other accelerated learning methods (particularly imagery [see Section #11]), into the learning process. Such mental "priming" utilizing imagery, music, and relaxation fosters and supplements the power of the subliminal message (see Section #18).

Extensive legal data base searchs indicate that no judicial rulings, federal or state laws, nor federal or state regulations exist regulating the use of audio subliminal messages (Ref. 23). However, there are legal implications for their use. The author strongly recommends that those using subliminals do so only after obtaining participants' written permission (see Appendix D for a sample permission form). Doing so addresses the potential legal doctrine that the public must have "reasonable access" to message content.

The author further recommends that, once permission statements have been obtained, they should be kept on file for the maximum statute of limitations (usually six years) for the states in which participants reside. Additionally, consenting participants should be given and advised to keep their own copies of their permission statements. Retaining these documents minimizes the risk of lawsuit over the issue, eg, as mind control without the consent of the participant (as occurred in early 1990 in the recording industry).

During the 1980s, Utah legislators submitted a bill regarding the use of subliminal messages. The bill was not enacted, but its wording had an impact on the issue. The proposed bill stated that subliminal communication is an invasion of a person's privacy unless:

1. The person consents to use of subliminal communication, and the parties using subliminal communication can present proof of such consent
2. The parties sponsoring subliminal communication:
    (a) Provide the individual, upon request, with the an actual listing of the message content of the subliminal communication being requested
    (b) Conspicuously display the exact wording of the subliminal messages used, and such wording is easily legible

If subliminals are to be used in a group context, each member of the group must sign a permission form or allowance must be made for non-consenting participants to leave the room when subliminal messages are being presented.

Participants usually consent if the process of obtaining permission is properly conducted. Rarely do individuals withhold permission.

Guidelines for Consumers

Consumers should consider the following guidelines before purchasing and/or using subliminal tapes:

- Seek ethical tape production and reproduction companies that provide message content
- Compare the message content with guidelines for constructing affirmations (see Section #13) to determine their effectiveness
- If messages occur within music, compare subliminals with guidelines for effectiveness, especially tempo (see Section #15)
- Check the duplication speed of the tape, ie, *real time, near real time*, or *fast-speed*. Real time and near real time duplication speeds are preferred; fast-speed duplication causes a loss of some high and low frequencies and of harmonics, necessary components in the creation of a relaxed state
- Be aware of and avoid "time compression" in the delivery of subliminals within tapes, which accelerate verbal communication (similar to playing a 33 rpm record at 78 rpm speed); research indicates that messages should be delivered slowly, methodically, and in cadence with the music into which they are embedded

Audio Subliminal Effectiveness:
A Re-Evaluation

Often audiocassette subliminal products are not effective because:

- Messages are improperly worded and do not follow guidelines for construction of affirmations (see Section 13)
- The selected music and/or sound detracts from rather than enhances subliminal messages (see Section 15)
- Messages are technically improperly embedded into the music and/or sound (as in time compression)
- Key components of communication are lost during fast-speed tape duplications

Because much research on the effectiveness of subliminals is conducted using instruments (taped products) that are seriously flawed, results of many studies are unreliable, invalid, and inconclusive. Research results and study instruments can be deemed valid only when:

- Product standards are met
- Subjects perceive such products as placebos
- Subjects use imagery and other related skills — ie, affirmations, music, relaxation

Resources: Section #35, No. 1, 11, 16; see Section 36, Ref 45 for a listing of companies that offer subliminal products

References: 1, 23, 43, 45

#15 Music

Definitions

Sound is mechanical radiant energy that is transmitted by longitudinal pressure waves and is perceived by the sense of hearing. Pressure waves are measured in decibels, the units used to express the relative loudness of sounds. One decibel equals approximately the smallest degree of difference of loudness ordinarily detectable by the human ear, whose range includes about 130 decibels on a scale for which one decibel correlates with the faintest audible sound.

Noise, though it is usually noticeably loud, harsh, or discordant, is defined as sound that lacks agreeable musical quality, regardless of its volume. As unwanted sound, it is a psychological as well as a physical phenomenon.

Music is the combination and organization of vocal or instrumental sounds possessing harmony, rhythm, and melody to produce a unified composition having structure and continuity. Described as agreeable sound, music is often referred to as the language of the emotions.

Physiological Impacts of Sound

Research has indicated that hypertension, often associated with high levels of stress, is increased by loud and sustained noise and that long-term exposure to sound above 90 decibels can result in hearing loss. Some examples of everyday sounds and their decibel levels/ranges are:

- Live rock music, amplified .... 90 to 130
- A screaming child .... 90 to 115
- An alarm clock 80
- A dripping faucet 40
- Rush-hour traffic............................ 75 to 85
- A power lawn mower .... 100 to 105
- Vacuum cleaner .... 70 to 75

Physiological Impacts of Music

Music impacts the body both positively and negatively (much like stress [see Sections #6 and #16]). Because instrumental music is non-verbal, it moves directly through the auditory cortex (see Section #7) to the limbic system (the center of emotional responses), where it induces the release into the body of endorphins (opiate-like chemicals that relieve pain and produce euphoric feelings).

Music also impacts:
- The heart, which normally beats between 70 and 80 times per minute but which adjusts to synchronize with music tempos
- The respiratory rate, which synchronizes with music tempos
- Blood pressure
- Stomach contractions
- Levels of stress hormones in the blood (high levels appear to suppress the immune system)
- Physical reactions to stress:
  - Fast tempos generally heighten arousal
  - Slow tempos generally help lower physical reactions to stress
  - Brain wave rhythms, which synchronize with musical tempos. One study demonstrated that, at 60 beats per minute, all

four brain waves become proportionately balanced. Lozanov discovered that 60 beat per minute music, particularly Baroque classical music, facilitated accelerated learning

Positive Impacts

Ornstein and Sobel (Ref 32) reviewed the literature and found that:

- Classical music played before, during, and after surgery:
  - Reduces patients' anxiety
  - Lessens patients' pain
  - Reduces the need for pre- and post-operative medication
  - Accelerates healing
- Combined with Lamaze birthing methods, appropriate music reduces the duration of labor by as much as two hours
- Music is often used in the treatment of patients whose illnesses involve strong emotional components

Such evidence, combined with the fact of interactions between the mind and body, suggests that illness should be treated holistically. For every illness, there are both physiological and psychological components, the former being the natural organic progression of disease and the latter being the emotional "dis-ease" of the patient. Correctly used, music can enhance the healing of both components of illness.

Because of their awareness of the impact of music, many physicians play Baroque music while performing surgery.

Even plants have been proven to grow especially quickly and to remain in excellent health in an environment of classical music.

"Music medicine" cuts across all health care disciplines. Considering the evidence, it seems logical to include its use in the fostering of environments conducive to healing whenever possible.

Negative Impacts

The negative consequences of music are as emphatic as the positive. Plants, for example, wither in the environment of rock music (which can range from 90 to 130 decibels). Some patients have been found to be addicted to music; Halpern (Ref 21) asserts that sound and rhythm can be as addictive as any known drug, and Tame (Ref 44) interviewed rock musicians who believe that they can create audience hysteria at will through their music.

Tame also cites 76 documented cases of *musiogenic epilepsy* (Ref 44), a condition in which music causes seizures. Halpern cites the results of a major study which reveals that, when rock music is played during physical exercise, 90 percent of participants lose strength and muscle coordination.

Shrill sounds projected into liquid protein have been found to coagulate the protein. Tame cites experiments in which a raw egg placed on stage during a rock concert has "cooked" to a hardened state by the end of the concert.

Though current efforts are under way in several states to regulate the lyrics of rock music, the author contends that the greatest negative effects come not from lyrics but from the high volumes, fast rhythms, and possibly subliminals contained in the music (see Section #14).

The Impact of Music upon Learning

Various research studies, including Lozanov's (see Section #3), indicate that when properly used, music facilitates and accelerates learning and health.

Music impacts directly on the limbic system. Various research studies indicate that music facilitates and accelerates learning. Music was an integral component for Lozanov (Section 3).

Music impacts directly upon the limbic system. Recall that one of the three primary functions of the limbic system is that of information processing, storage, and retrieval (Section 6). Music also appeals to the emotions, another limbic system function, and is known to be strongly *associative*, evoking *imagery* (Section 11).

Recall the two definitions of music, above. Recall that the limbic system is interconnected by the *hippocampal commisure* (Sections 7 and 10), connected to the right and left brain hemispheres (Sections 7 and 11) and that the right and left brain hemispheres are connected by the *corpus callosum* (Section 8). Music facilitates, supplements these natural interconnections, assisting the hemispheres in coordinating their functions, in working together "in harmony."

Music also facilitates the creation of alpha brain waves, a pattern which aids in stress-reduction and enhanced learning (see Section #8).

The three types of music and sound that accelerate learning and healing are:
- Classical music
- New Age music
- Environmental sounds

Classical Music

Lozanov (see Section #3) found that learning could be facilitated when accompanied by Baroque and classical musical selections having *andante* (moderately slow; a quarter-note tempo of 40 to 72 beats per minute), *adagio* (slower than andante; a quarter-note tempo of 50 to 76 beats per minute), *largo* (slower than adagio; a quarter-note tempo of 42 to 66 beats per minute) tempos. These tempos *approximate* the 60-beats-per-minute range that Lozanov found to be a key tempo for the enhancement of accelerated learning.

Researchers of Lozanov's methods discovered that, though the physiological states produced in participants who listened to classical music of the 60-beats-per-minute range was unlike meditation, the physiological effects were similar, including:

- Lowered blood pressure
- Reduced breathing rates
- Reduced heart rates

The participants were relaxed yet alert and were able to focus and concentrate; their EEG brain wave patterns (see Section #8) displayed an increase in alpha (associated with alertness) and a decrease in delta and theta (associated with drowsiness) patterns.

These same participants, in spite of their intense mental activity, also displayed an overall decrease of beta brain waves, a pattern often associated with states of anxiety and prominent in the appropriate brain hemisphere involved with the mental task at hand (see Section #8).

Composers spanning the Baroque period of classical music (approximately 1600-1750, including J.S. Bach, Scarlatti, Handel, Haydn, Vivaldi,

Corelli, Pachelbel) did not write "song titles" as we would term them today. Rather, their "titles" were their "signature": the "names" of the tempos were "instructions" to the conductor as to "how fast" to play the composition:

Largo: "very slow"
Adagio: "quite slow"
Andante: "a walking pace"

When you select this type of music for purchase, look for these "song titles". They shall be listed. (see also Appendix E for a listing of musical recommendations involving classical music this writer utilizes in formalized training.)

New Age Music

New Age music is a growing segment of the recording industry, with radio stations across the country devoting programs to this type of music.

No specific definition of New Age music has been determined; even composers and musicians of the genre cannot agree on a definition. However, there are a few common characteristics that music of this type seems to share:

- New Age music is primarily non-verbal and is designed to be as unobtrusive to the listener as possible
- New Age musical rhythms are not "stop-anapestic" — ie, there is no beginning, middle, or end. Much popular music contains this stop-anapestic rhythm, which consists of a "short-short-long-pause" pattern. This pattern was the one found associated with the physical workout research study cited by Halpern, above
- New Age music is designed to foster a state of relaxation, enabling the listener to tran-

scend time and space (via the right hemisphere's function of timelessness [see Sections #7 and #9]). (Appendices E and F list selections whose titles allude to this characteristic)
- Much New Age music approximates the 60 beats per minute tempo
- New Age music is cross-cultural, reinforcing the quality of transcendence, (transcending time and space) by utilizing instruments of various cultures
- New Age musical compositions often incorporate synthesized special effects with instrumental and environmental sounds

Environmental Sounds

The author notes that an overwhelming majority of participants of his training programs find themselves imaging outdoor locations when they are asked to create a relaxation sanctuary (see Section #18), with some indicating that, although they consciously selected an indoor site, they found themselves mentally outdoors. Additionally, most report an association with water, regardless of the indoor or outdoor location.

This is no accident. The body, naturally relaxed, vibrates at a rate of approximately 7.8 to 8 cycles per second, approximating the rate of the alpha brain wave state (see Section #8); geophysicists have demonstrated that the earth vibrates at this same frequency. Human beings automatically become attuned to nature and its harmonies when in a relaxed state.

Research has concluded that a state of relaxation is promoted by environmental sounds, such as:

- The ocean surf and seagulls
- A trickling stream
- Birds singing
- Crickets chirping
- The environment of a tropical rain forest

The author recommends creating and maintaining a state of relaxation by playing either classical or New Age music simultaneously with an environmental sound tape that is associated with one's relaxation sanctuary. (see Section #18).

Musical Notes

Two musical "camps" have emerged in the field of accelerated learning. Those in one camp advocate the strict application of classical music for learning enhancement; those in the other advocate New Age music because it has the advantage of promoting relaxation without focusing upon the familiarity of much of classical music. It must be noted, however, that, the popularizing of New Age compositions shall lead to the "familiarity" argument being raised against New Age music as well.

Probably, the greatest learning enhancement comes from the use of both music types, supplemented with recordings of environmental sounds.

Health care professionals do a disservice to clients, staff, and patients if they allow stress management/wellness consultants to omit the use of appropriate music as a part of such program services as:

- Learning and training methodology
- Relaxation skills development
- Training workshop subject content
- Technical assistance services

Health care professionals also deprive themselves if they do not incorporate "sound nutrition" into their own health maintenance and wellness programs and their own learning and study processes. (See Section #35 for resource information regarding the effective use of music in accelerated learning methodology.)

References: 10, 21, 33, 35, 38, 43, 44

#16 Relaxation

The Relaxation Response

The limbic system evokes the "fight or flight" response when the body is under extreme tension (see Section #6). The short-term advantage of this response is that it helps to insure survival, ie, the body is prepared and poised for action when danger is perceived. Under long-term chronic stress, however, this response, especially because of its intensity, impairs health and suppresses the immune system, causing bodily deterioration.

At issue is whether the response to stress must always be an either/or proposition. Must the response be the extreme "fight or flight" only, or are there less extreme and/or alternative ways in which the body can react to long- or short-term stress?

Dr. Herbert Benson of Harvard University helped pioneer a learned response, termed the relaxation response, that serves as an alternative reaction to stressful situations (Ref 4). Benson's studies revealed that this learned relaxation response evokes more positive physiological responses than the "fight or flight" phenomenon; these include:

- A lowering of the breathing rate
- A decrease in oxygen consumption
- A shift in brain wave patterns from beta to alpha rhythms, thereby creating a relaxed yet alert mental state
- A decrease in blood flow to the muscles and a simultaneous increase in blood flow to the skin and brain, which produce feelings of warmth

The physiological changes produced by the relaxation response are similar to those brought about by appropriate music (see Section #15). Both produce relaxed mental alertness, a critical factor in accelerated learning.

Various types of mental concentration and skill development (see below) also can bring about these same physiological changes; mental concentration acts upon the limbic system to create the relaxation response.

The Relationships of Stress, Learning, and Relaxation

Stress and anxiety are associated with a high-beta "brain print" (see Sections #6 and #8). In preparing the body to meet crisis situations, the limbic system, as a result of stress, causes the senses to be honed, the mind to be focused, and the body to be poised for action. These reactions cannot be sustained long-term, however.

Stress researcher Dr. Hans Seyle classified physical reactions to stress as the *general adaptation syndrome* (GAS), a three-stage phenomenon:

- Alarm Reaction—A reaction to the stressor in which the brain prepares the body via the "fight or flight" response
- Resistance—An increase above normal levels in bodily resistance to the stressor
- Exhaustion—A reaction in which, if the stressor does not diminish:
  - The body's store of energy becomes exhausted
  - Resistance to the stressor decreases
  - The probability of illness increases

The GAS principle can be applied to overall performance as well as to bodily responses. As stress and anxiety increase, so initially does performance. After a period of time, however, performance — even basic learning — decreases (because of exhaustion) if the anxiety level continues to increase. This principle comes into play whenever excessive stress and/or panic set in. For example, though they may be highly experienced, hunters or backpackers can become lost in the woods and forget how to use their equipment when faced with particularly stressful situations.

Learning

The GAS principle of responses to stress can also be applied to learning. As individuals concentrate intently for long periods and create stress by doing so, they become less relaxed and their performance ultimately declines.

Lozanov found that the opposite is also true, ie, learners have as much difficulty concentrating when they are profoundly relaxed as when they are profoundly stressed (see Section #3). In a profoundly relaxed state, learners become drowsy and inattentive and their capacity for learning diminishes acutely.

As a means of avoiding these extremes, Lozanov's methods of attaining the relaxed yet alert state (see Section #2) bring the learner to the optimal point of alertness *without* stress and to a state of relaxation *without* inattentiveness, even during intense language training.

Relaxation

The same methods used to create the relaxed yet alert mental state necessary for accelerated learning are recommended for relaxation therapy for the treatment of hypertension. The methods include:

- Yoga, especially Hatha Yoga
- Progressive muscle relaxation
- Abdominal breathing
- Transcendental Meditation (TM)
- Isotonic exercise (active muscle movement, eg, aerobic exercise)
- Autogenic relaxation (self-regulation through verbal cues and imagery)
- Biofeedback

As previously noted, all relaxation methods are more effective when combined with imagery (see Section #11) and appropriate music (see Section #15). Specific exercises combining the techniques of relaxation, music, and imagery are noted in Section #18.

References: 4, 8, 14, 35, 39

#17 Creating a Learning Environment

The Four-Step Self-Study Process
The four-step self-study process of accelerated learning is described in Sections #17 through #20. Effective learning results (see Section #4) should be realized if this process is followed sequentially (Figure 17.1) and if the accelerated learning methods described in Sections #10 through #16 are used correctly. Special considerations for older learners are noted in Section #27.

It is important that the proper learning environment be incorporated into and maintained throughout each step of the study process if accelerated learning methods are to be effective. The proper physical learning environment should be established before actual study begins so that the study area provides the most effective ambience for learners from the beginning of the process.

Critical factors involved in creating a proper learning environment are as follows:
- Interruptions
- Room temperature
- Food and drug intake
- Lighting
- Accelerated learning methods

Interruptions and Room Temperature
The work/study area should be isolated enough to free the learner from interruptions. It should also, in terms of temperature, be comfortable for the group or individual.

Food and Drug Intake

Be aware of the need for concentration and focus. There is anxiety associated with learning. This becomes more acute if testing is involved. Under tension, the brain slows down the digestive system. Consequently, food takes longer to digest.

If you are on prescribed medication, know the side effects. Does the medication cause drowsiness, thus interfering with concentration?

Lighting

An early 1980s Harris poll stated that 85 percent of respondents identified lighting as the number one factor in on-the-job comfort. For the learning environment, study areas should be:

- Provided with natural lighting when possible
- Provided with full spectrum lighting if natural lighting is not feasible
- Void of direct overhead fluorescent lighting, if possible

Study areas should be near windows in order to make use of natural lighting, if possible; research indicates that natural lighting in the workplace makes people feel better.

If natural lighting is not feasible, full spectrum lighting (fluorescent bulbs which simulate natural light and provide ultraviolet light and visible parts of the spectrum) should be used. Some studies suggest that full spectrum lighting may improve visual acuity and contribute to productivity (seasonal affective disorder patients are treated with such lighting). A negative effect of full spectrum lighting is the potential association of ultraviolet light with skin cancer; more research needs to be done in this area.

FIGURE 17.1 – The Four-Step Accelerated Learning Self-Study Process

1. Creating a stress-free learning environment
2. Relaxation Exercises
3. Active Study
4. "R & R": Review and Reinforcement
   Initial Review: Active and Passive (including visual/verbal review)
   Subsequent Review Periods

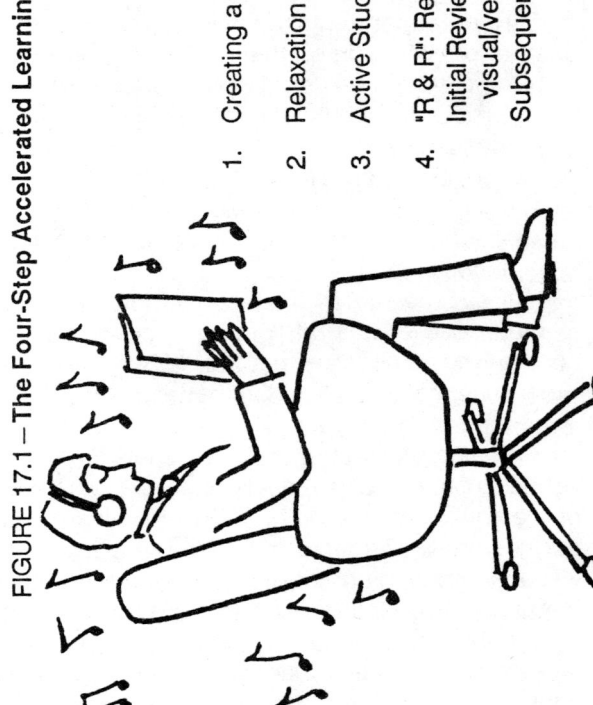

Direct overhead fluorescent lighting should be avoided. Fluorescent lighting flickers approximately 120 times per second. Video display terminal operators complain that such lighting causes fatigue. Other health impairments associated with fluorescent lighting include:

- Muscle soreness
- Headache
- Eye strain

Some other recommendations for the control of light in the study area include use of:

- Ambient indirect fluorescent lighting
- Task lighting
- Subdued tones for wall colors

Most environmental psychologists and lighting experts recommend ambient indirect fluorescent lighting. Because the indirect light reflects off the ceiling, contrast ratios (ie, the contrast in brightness between an object and its background) are reduced, as are the associated physiological symptoms. A negative effect is that, because of the calm environment created by indirect lighting, external stimuli often seem noisier and are more bothersome than when they occur in other lighting environments.

Task lighting, ie, light provided only to the area of work (eg, a high-intensity desk lamp), has been found to:

- Reduce glare (see Sections #12 and #27)
- Conserve energy and lower energy costs
- Create a comfortable work/study environment

If computers are used, the colors of the walls (especially bright white) may cause eye strain. Such brightness forces the eye to refocus and readjust each time the worker looks away from and back to the computer terminal.

Accelerated Learning Methods

Accelerated learning methods should be incorporated into the work/study area and the self-study process, including:

- Music/sound (see Section #5)
- Peripherals (see Section #12)
- Learning affirmations (see Section #13)
- Subliminals (see Section #14)
- Imagery (see Section #11)
- Relaxation (see Section #16)
- Learning style preferences (see Section #10)

References: 3, 31, 43, 46

NOTES

#18 Relaxation Exercises

After the comfortable, stress-free work/study environment is prepared, the learner should take time for relaxation before beginning study (see Section #16). The exercises offered here, developed by Swartz and Associates (see Section #35), are extremely beneficial to accelerated learning and stress management and are intended to foster the relaxation response (see Section #16).

The author strongly recommends that the reader study this section in full before practicing any of the exercises.

Exercise I – Creating a Relaxation Sanctuary

This exercise is intended to create a mental place of relaxation, by using physical and imaginative (sensory) means. The steps of the exercise follow:

1. Play appropriate background music (see Section #15) during the exercise. Kobialka's *Timeless Motion,* a New Age composition (see Section #15 and Appendix F), is strongly recommended.
2. As the music plays, decide on a relaxation "sanctuary" that you would find appealing (ie, the most relaxing place and situation you can imagine); write a description of this place, placing it at the top center of a piece of unlined paper.
3. On the same page, below and to the right, list the six senses:
    TASTE
    HEARING
    SMELL
    TOUCH
    VISION
    MOTION

4. Next to each sense, list a few key descriptive words and/or phrases to indicate how you would use each sense in your relaxation sanctuary. Use present tense (see Section #13) language.
5. Create mental images for the descriptions listed. If desired, note the images on the same page (see Section #11).
6. Take a few deep breaths and close your eyes. Recall your relaxation sanctuary and as many of your mental images as possible.

Exercise II — The "22 Count" Breathing Exercise

The purpose of this exercise is to create a balanced relaxed yet alert state, the optimal state for enhanced learning. It also offers practice in abdominal breathing and can be done in combination with Exercise I.

Preparation

The learner is advised to read all instructions before beginning this exercise. To prepare for the exercise, the learner is to:

1. Play appropriate background music, such as Kobialka's *Timeless Motion* or *Dream Passage* (see Appendix F) or recordings of environmental sounds that are associated with your relaxation sanctuary (see Section #15), during the exercise.
2. Sit comfortably on a chair or sofa or on the floor. Do not lie on the floor; doing so may cause you to become drowsy and lose mental focus. Why? Any appropriate relaxation technique and medication properly done may create increased energy. The body drained of en-

ergy, now experiences energy flowing through it. It's a "cultural shock" for the body. Drowsiness and sleep may thus result. The goal of this exercise is to create a relaxed yet alert state; sleep negates that goal.
3. Loosen and/or remove your tie, constricting jewelry, and shoes. Place your feet flat on the floor (if you are sitting on a chair or sofa). Rest your hands on your thighs.
4. Become aware of your body touching the surface on which you are sitting and of your clothing touching your body; this awareness is called focusing or centering. The position of your body should manifest the self-centering that occurs mentally and emotionally within it (this is the true meaning of self-centeredness).

Diaphragmatic Breathing

As Lozanov noted, the heart rate, blood pressure, and breathing rate involuntarily synchronize with musical rhythms, creating alpha brain wave states that produce relaxation responses, diminish stress, promote healing, and enhance learning (see Section #15). Playing appropriate music during breathing exercises aids in the achievement of targeted breathing and heart rates.

Rhythmic breathing is key to relaxation training and accelerated learning; the key to rhythmic breathing is diaphragmatic (abdominal) breathing.

The diaphragm, a large muscle situated just below the lungs, separates the lungs from the abdominal cavity. When inhaling, the stomach extends outward and the diaphragm contracts, pulling air into the lungs (Figure 18.1); when exhaling, the stomach falls inward and the diaphragm is relaxed, pushing air out of the lungs (Figure 18.1). This synchronization is established by the deep sigh that initiates the diaphragmatic breathing exercise.

Diaphragmatic breathing provides the brain with increased oxygen (ie, at least eight times the volume of chest inhalations, which provide approximately 500 centimeters of air), giving the body more energy. It also fosters relaxation and health. A study by Harvard University's Health Maintenance Organization (HMO) revealed that patients trained in relaxation skills and diaphragmatic breathing reduced their number of regular clinic visits by approximately 50 percent.

Dr. Joan Borysenko, director of Boston's Beth Israel Hospital's Mind/Body Clinic and instructor of medicine at Harvard Medical School (Ref 7, 8), describes the steps of diaphragmatic breathing:

1. Sit comfortably, become self-centered, and place one hand on the stomach.
2. Sigh deeply through your mouth, feeling the stomach "fall in" slightly; gently contract the stomach muscles slightly to exhale the last bit of air.
3. With your hand still on your stomach, close your mouth and inhale through your nose, feeling the stomach expand. If the abdomen remains flat, you are breathing from your chest rather than your diaphragm; if this is the case, repeat steps 2 and 3, this time using the stomach muscles to push outward.
4. Feel the stomach extend as the lower and upper portions of your lungs fill with air.
5. Exhale through your nose, emptying the lungs and diaphragm; slightly contract the stomach muscles if necessary.

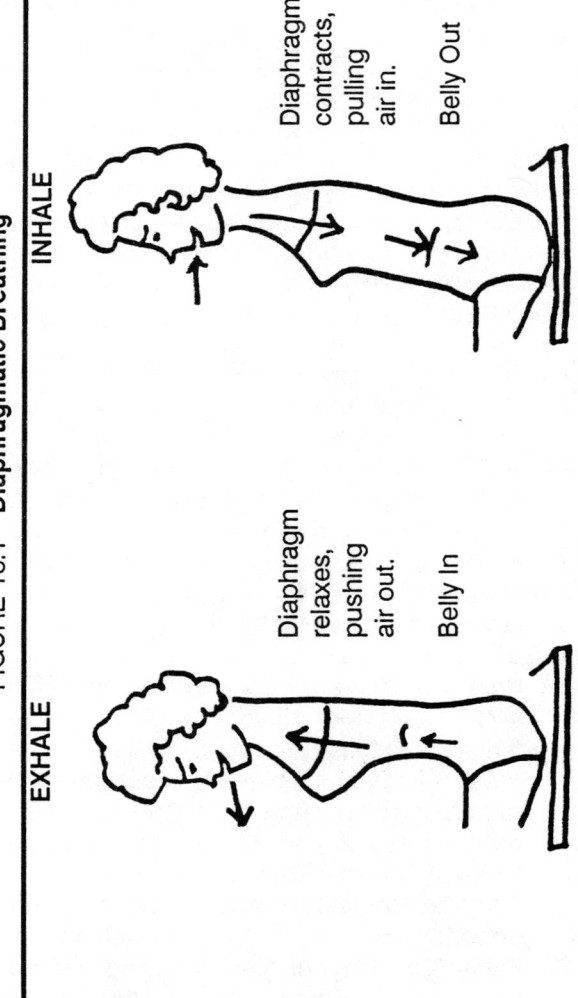

FIGURE 18.1 – **Diaphragmatic Breathing**

6. Feel the abdomen fall as air leaves your lungs
7. Continue breathing in this manner, feeling your abdomen rise and fall, your shoulders move up and down, and your body rock slightly
8. Breathe normally and begin study

The "22-Count" Breathing Exercise

The learner is encouraged to use diaphragmatic breathing in the "22-count" breathing exercise. The steps of the exercise follow:

1. Play appropriate music during the exercise. Dim or turn off artificial lighting.
2. Sit comfortably in the study area (the established learning environment).
3. Become self-centered; recall your relaxation sanctuary and the mental (sensory) images you created for it to assist you in becoming self-centered.
4. Inhale abdominally, holding your breath for 22 counts (counting slowly) or as long as possible.
5. Exhale.
6. Repeat steps 4 and 5 two more times.
7. Close your eyes and breath normally.
8. Imagine yourself in your relaxation sanctuary; try to feel as many of the senses associated with it as possible.
9. Slowly return your thoughts to the reality of the study area. Wiggle your fingertips and toes, stretch your arms and legs, and feel the chair you are sitting in, the clothes you are wearing, and the floor your feet are touching. Become aware of the sounds of your environment.
10. Open your eyes slowly. Stand and stretch.

Additional Notes

The learner may wish to play subliminal tapes with messages that approximate the intent of the "22-count" breathing exercise while performing the exercise, or to record and play his/her own audiocassettes of the steps of the "22-count" breathing exercise. (It is important to the effectiveness of a tape that the narrative be recorded in the learner's own voice; this reinforces the learner's taking responsibility for his/her own relaxation and learning.)

During exercise, the learner is encouraged to allow his/her thoughts to flow without inhibition or interruption. The objective is to slow the thought process (aided by the slow, rhythmic cadence used in counting to 22) but still allow a free flow of thoughts.

Attempting to force an emptying of the mind of all thoughts is not encouraged. Because such a mental state is difficult to attain, the attempt to achieve it often causes the very tension that the learner is trying to relieve.

For the same reasons, forcing relaxation also is discouraged. After failing at forced relaxation, learners often become frustrated and experience feelings of guilt when considering the reasons for their failure, thus, increasing rather than relieving anxiety.

To avoid such frustrations and tension-creating situations, the author recommends that learners focus on breathing exercises and creating relaxation sanctuaries, activities that foster comfortable, stress-free learning environments and attitudes.

Physiological Effects of Relaxation Exercises

Learners may initially experience a few negative side effects of relaxation exercises, including:

- Temporary swelling of the fingers — This results from increased energy in the body and will subside soon after exercises are completed. Learners may wish to remove rings before beginning exercises
- Tingling or twitching of arms and/or legs — This is due to a release of pent-up energy
- Slight tension or headache — These effects may occur in those for whom focusing on relaxation:
  - Is an "in-tense" challenge. Some individuals force their eyes closed while concentrating on relaxing. This can cause physical strain and tension that can result in headache
  - Creates anxiety and/or fear. Lower limbic, left-dominant information processors and learners (see Section #10) are especially apprehensive about risk-taking or making changes in learning styles
  - Is so foreign that the body reacts to the increased energy surge created by the relaxation exercises. The brain creates energy (see Section #8); thus, the body is electric

To aid relaxation, learners may wish to repeat the following sets of affirmations prior to exercise:

- I am relaxed yet alert
- I am feeling refreshed and at peace
- I am free of tension
- I am free of negative thoughts and feelings
- I am relaxation being

- I am harmony being
- I am ease-ment being
- I am physical health being
- I am mental and emotional health being
- I am relaxed

Professional Assistance

Learners desiring advanced training in relaxation therapies (eg, meditation and yoga) are encouraged to seek assistance from qualified professionals rather than attempt to learn these therapies on their own. As with all accelerated learning/healing methods, such therapies are intended to supplement rather than substitute for medical treatment regimens.

References: 7, 8, 43

NOTES

#	Topic	Section
1.	Definition of Accelerated Learning	Background
2.	Characteristics of Accelerated Learning	
3.	History of Accelerated Learning	
4.	Results of Accelerated Learning Implementation	
5.	The Brain: A Working Model	Brain/Mind Research Findings
6.	The Limbic System: Stress and Learning	
7.	Left and Right Cerebral Hemispheres	
8.	Brain Waves and Their Characteristics	
9.	The Holographic Brain	
10.	Brain Dominance and Learning Styles: An Overview	Methods
11.	Imagery	
12.	Peripheral Visual Aids	
13.	Learning Affirmations	
14.	Subliminals	
15.	Music	
16.	Relaxation	
17.	Creating a Learning Environment	4-Step Self Study Process
18.	Relaxation Exercises	

4-Step Self Study Process (con't)	Active Study	19.
	Review and Reinforcement	20.
Health Care Training Model	Health Care Training Model: An Overview	21.
	Creating a Stress-Free Learning Environment	22.
	Relaxation Exercises	23.
	Orchestrated Learning: Active and Passive	24.
	Elaboration and Reinforcement	25.
	Experiential Learning	26.
	Special Needs of the Older Adult Learner	27.
Appendices	Appendix A – Brain Dominance Occupational Profiles	28.
	Appendix B – Brain Dominance Occupational Profiles: Narrative Descriptions	29
	Appendix C – Format Guidelines for Creating a Text	30.
	Appendix D – Permission Form: Learning Affirmation Audio Subliminals	31.
	Appendix E – Musical Learning Notes	32.
	Appendix F – New Age Music	33.
	Appendix G – Active Learning Narrative Dialogue: An Example	34.
Sources	Resources	35.
	References	36.

#19 Active Study

At this stage of the four-step self-study process, the learner should be ready to begin actual study. It should be noted that every person's study method is uniquely his/her own, fitting his/her own personality, characteristics, experiences, and needs.

Although the nature of the material to be learned often dictates the approach that is taken in acquiring knowledge and skills, *how* a person studies usually determines what he learns. However, a few generalizations can be applied to all learners and learning and should be considered in facilitating active study:

- The sequence of study steps of the four-step accelerated learning self-study process may seem to delay actual study, but their use actually saves time in the long run. Though educational research has not confirmed a direct correlation between the amount of study time and amount of knowledge learned, considerable resources confirm a direct correlation between accelerated learning methods and acquired learning and recall (see Sections #3 and #4)
- As accelerated learning methods and self-study processes are practiced, they become second nature to the learner and thus require less time to perform
- Used simultaneously with relaxation exercises (see Section #18), the learner integrates wellness programming into his learning and may find that his actual study time for acquiring knowledge and skills is reduced. With this method, there should be no need for learners

to expend large amounts of energy "cramming" on the night before a major test

The steps of the active study process follow:

1. Organize yourself:
   - Assemble necessary supplies and equipment before you begin actual study
2. Know your learning style preferences (see Section #10) and plan your study accordingly. If you haven't assessed your learning style, through the HBDI (see Section #10) or another psychological learning assessment battery, answer the following basic questions:
   - In which subject areas do I excel?
   - Who were my favorite teachers? Why?
   - What is my profession? Is it my natural-preference?

   Interpret your answers in terms of brain dominance theories (see Section #10) to determine your learning style preferences
3. Create an accelerated learning environment before you begin actual study (see Section #17):
   - Perform relaxation exercises (see Section #18)
   - Create your relaxation sanctuary; include in it associated scenic pictures and/or posters
   - Maintain these peripherals in your learning environment
4. Prepare for active study:
   - Begin playing the music or environmental sounds you have chosen for your relaxation sanctuary (see Section #15):
     - If study material is new information, try a subliminal tape (see Section #14)
     - Use 90-minute tapes to avoid interrup-

tions caused by having to constantly switch tapes and/or sides of a tape. 90 minute tapes contain two sides of approximately 45 minutes to each side. 45 minutes also approximates an appropriate study period length (see Number 6, below)
- Recall study techniques taught by past instructors which differentiate reading for pleasure and reading for study and retention, such as:
  - Questioning yourself about:
    - The purpose of the assignment
    - How the purpose corresponds to coverage of material in class
    - How the purpose corresponds to the teacher's instructions
    - What the teacher's instructions include
    - The contents of the study material. Rather than immediately beginning to read:
      - Scan the material to determine what is being said. There is no rule stating that material must be read from page one sequentially through to the end
      - Review introductions, summaries, and conclusions to get an overview of the material
      - Review headings, subheadings, and captions of charts and figures to determine their relationship to the main points
      - Determine how the reading material relates to your class notes
      - Look at the author's style, noting especially where and how key points are introduced in a paragraph

5. Begin active study:
   - Highlight material as you read, creating your own notes in the process
   - Incorporate the left/right note-study system (see Section #11) as you read; if you do not actually create imagery at this point, at least make note of key words, definitions, concepts, etc. This will save study time later
   - Use mind-mapping (see Section #11) to illustrate how bits of information are related
6. Continue active study for an appropriate period of time; the length of the study period will depend on:
   - Your attention span
   - Your comfort level
   - Your level of tension and anxiety
   - The nature of the material being studied

   Buzan (Ref 11) recommends a study period of approximately 40 minutes. Research indicates that material studied at the beginning and end of a study period is most easily recalled. A decline in recall occurs, especially for material studied during the mid-point of the process, if study periods are too lengthy
7. Pause for 15 to 20 minutes after an appropriate study period to perform a few physical stretching exercises. (The author recommends calling this period a "pause" rather than a "break" from study, since the mind, via the paraconscious senses, continues to absorb information presented in the peripheral visual aids during this time [see Section #2])

8. Resume study, taking a moment beforehand to:
   - Read your learning affirmations
   - Scan related peripherals
   - Focus on your relaxation sanctuary posters while taking one or two deep abdominal breaths (see Sections #17 and #18)
   - Repeat the study preparations (see above)

References: 11, 43

NOTES

#20 Review and Reinforcement

The last step of the four-step self-study process includes the initial review of study material and subsequent reinforcement.

Initial Review
The initial review of material involves:
- Active review
- Visual/verbal review
- Passive review

Active Review
For effective learning, active review is necessary soon after the active study period (see Section #19), since 80 percent of material initially learned is lost (for recall purposes) within 24 hours unless the material is reinforced (Ref 11). The steps of active review of material for subsequent recall follow:
1. Review the study material, creating imagery whenever appropriate and using the left/right note-study system for key words, definitions, concepts, etc. (see Section #11).
2. Mentally create three-dimensional images to help you associate and recall new terms. Remember that, since the brain is like a hologram (see Section #9), sensory integrations associated with your created images are critical to reinforcement of material learned
3. To enhance the transfer of information from short- to long-term memory, reinforce sensory integration (this occurs in the limbic system [see Section #6])
4. Use additional study methods to reinforce materials, such as:

- Mind-mapping (see Section #11)
- Creating a narrative dialogue (see Section #24) that contains the information to be recalled. (This is an excellent tool, whether accompanied by imagery or not, for an upper right-brain processor [see Section #10 and Appendix G], because it puts information into story form.)
- Creating your own audiocassette tape of key terms and definitions, sequential steps of a formula, etc. Points to consider when recording include:
  - Pacing and speech cadence, since the body synchronizes to the rhythm of the speech pattern (see Section #18):
    - Speak slowly
    - Pause between bits of information
    - To avoid monotony, vary your intonation and volume
  - Appropriate background music with tempos that enhance learning (see Section #15); classical music is recommended. Music with slightly faster tempos may accompany left/right note-taking (see Section #11 and Appendix E)

Visual/Verbal Review

For this review period, classical music with slower tempos is recommended. The steps of visual and verbal review of material for subsequent recall follow. These steps relate primarily to the Left-Right Note Study System found in Section 11.

1. Take one or two deep abdominal breaths; relax. (see Section #18)
2. Visually focus on each image you created during active review; pause.

3. Describe aloud the meaning of each image and the senses utilized while doing so, attempting to experience each sense as you name it; pause.
4. Look at the right side of the page to the term and definition depicted by each image. Vocalize each term and definition, pausing between them; pause.
5. Repeat steps 2 through 4 for each term, limiting the number of terms per cluster to seven (because short-term memory holds an average of seven pieces of new material at one time [see Section #6]).
6. If you have created a narrative dialogue, read it aloud, emphasizing those portions which contain key terms (especially those still unfamiliar). Incorporate the imagery exercises with the terms most unfamiliar to you.

Passive Review

During passive review, the learner is to be relaxed yet alert. Physically he is to be in a restful state, while mentally he is to be alert and capable of concentrating on the material at hand. The steps of passive review of material for subsequent recall follow:
1. Take one or two abdominal breaths, close your eyes, and become centered (focused) on the material to be learned.
2. Recall as many of the images and their associated terms and definitions as possible (within each seven-term cluster).
3. Open your eyes.
4. Review the material for any terms and/or definitions you may have omitted. Repeat the active and passive review steps for any omitted material.

5. If you created an audiocassette tape, listen to it with your eyes closed, first taking one or two deep abdominal breaths.

Subsequent Reinforcement

Generally, the more unfamiliar and foreign the subject matter is to your cognitive and learning style dominances (see Section #10), the greater the need for review.

The most critical review period for reinforcement occurs within 24 hours. Thereafter, reviews (about 10 minutes each) should be done at weekly intervals (Ref 11). These periodic structured reviews are necessary if material is to be kept in long-term memory. (Figure 20.1 illustrates the sequence that these reviews should take.)

The Consequences of Review

Some learning will always be lost, even though reviews are instituted; but the amount of learning lost is far less when active study and review are used than when they are not. Within the first 24 hours, the rate of loss may approximate 80% — *unless* review and reinforcement are undertaken (Ref 11).

Learning requires effort. At latest count, the adult education and training industry cost was estimated at $210 billion per year, an incredible human service expenditure, especially when seen in terms of an 80 percent waste and productivity loss if the learning is not reinforced by the institution of review periods and the inordinate amount of time learners must later spend "catching-up" (eg, cramming for examinations). Applied to in-

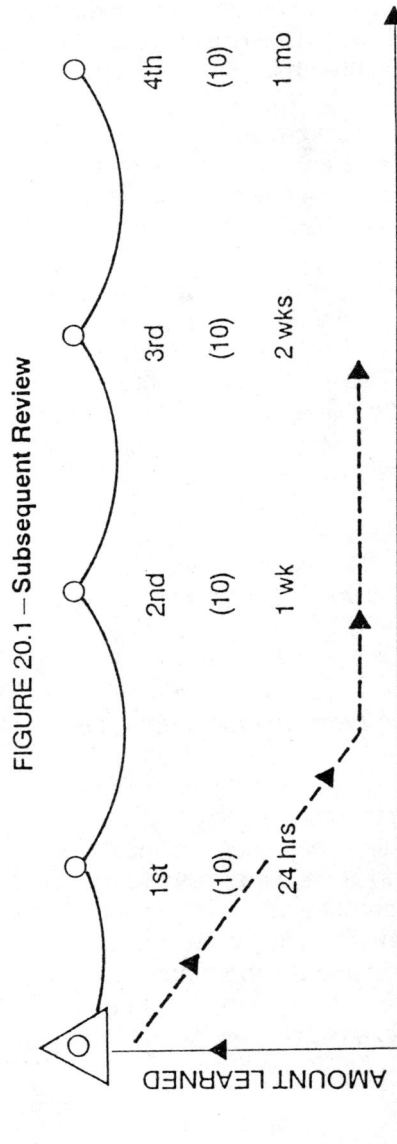

dustrial training, such waste costs enormous amounts of money and forces the country to play economic "catch-up" in order to be competitive in the world market.

A Zen management principle — "To save time, take time" — can be applied to this situation. A individual who takes time to review and reinforce his learning not only saves time but also learns and recalls more and reduces his stress, tension, and anxiety.

References: 11, 35, 43

#21 Health Care Training Model: An Overview

Accelerated learning techniques are currently being used in many training programs for health care professionals. Personnel are urged to take advantage of accelerated learning methods for the acceleration and enhancement of their own cognitive and psychomotor learning and physical well-being and so that they may apply these techniques to patient care for the enhancement of their patients' healing.

A model of the training process geared to the health care professional is illustrated in Figure 21.1. Patterned after the accelerated learning model developed by Morrissey (see Section #35, Resource 7) its steps and components parallel those for general accelerated learning. This health care training model attempts not to restate the fundamentals of accelerated learning but to incorporate them into the repertoire of skills and knowledge for health care professionals.

The specific steps and/or methods or techniques of accelerated learning that may be applied to the training of health care professionals with referrals to Sections for detailed discussions about them are:

- Creating a stress-free learning environment — Sections #17 and #22
- Relaxation exercises--Sections #16 and #23
- Orchestrated learning: Active and passive — Sections #19 and #24
- Elaboration and reinforcement — Sections #20 and #25
- Experiential learning — Section #26
- Special considerations for older adult learners — Section #27

Additional sources of information about training models and methods are listed in Section #35. This training model may also be used for business and industry; high school and post-secondary education; and for government

Training Assumptions Re-Examined

Too often false assumptions are made about the teaching and learning processes. For example, it is erroneously assumed that:

- People automatically learn when exposed to new content through appropriate training methods
- People automatically apply the skills and knowledge newly acquired in the classroom to their work tasks
- If people do not apply their newly-acquired skills to the workplace, it is because of constraints in the workplace that prevent the reinforcement of the classroom instruction
- Applied skills and knowledge automatically lead to greater productivity in the workplace

These assumptions are invalid in virtually every setting for a number a reasons. In particular for the health care industry, educators often rely on the health care system to provide on-the-job reinforcement of classroom training, but trainers and supervisors who are already overburdened have little or no time to provide such reinforcement. Also instructors often do not have the necessary skills (eg, training in accelerated learning techniques) to provide reinforcement, may not have learned the skills in question initially, or may not have reinforced their own learning and, thus, cannot recall the material themselves (see Section #20).

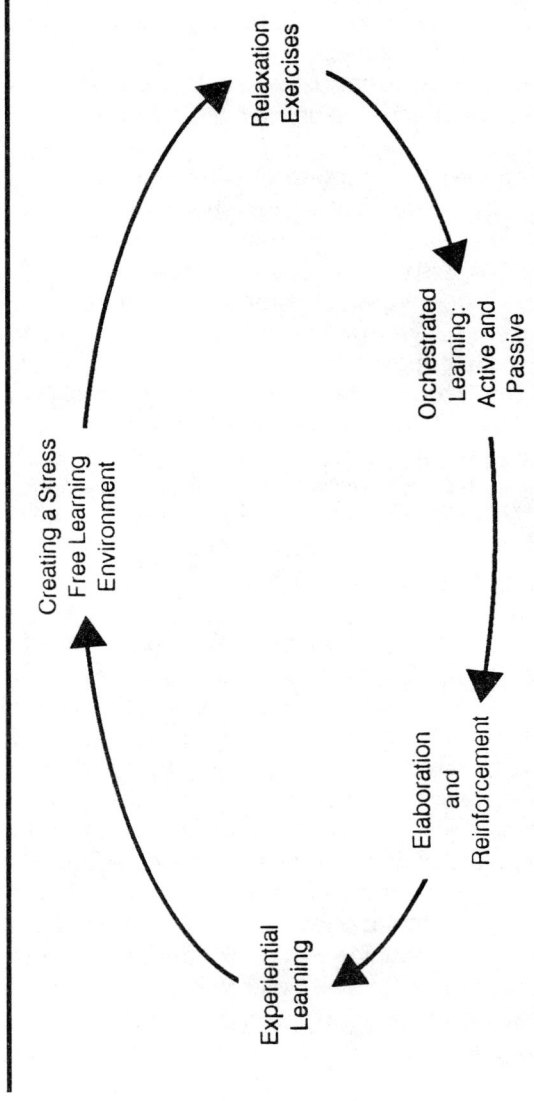

FIGURE 21.1 – The Accelerated Learning Health Care Training Cycle

Additionally, health care organizations usually are extremely understaffed, with no personnel available to provide reinforcement of training, and cannot provide a proper learning environment for ongoing training and/or reinforcement.

Changes need to be made in the continuing education and reinforcement of training if the health care industry is to progress. Neither the nation nor the schools, students, or patients can afford to have a health care professional fail his state board licensing examinations or to be incapable of performing a needed skill while on the job. In monetary terms, this situation is extremely costly, considering the enormous expenditures incurred for initial education, recruitment, interviewing, and hiring. More importantly, when a patient's well-being is a stake, the situation can become a matter of life and death.

References: 43

#22 Creating a Stress-Free Learning Environment

Purpose
A stress-free, relaxed learning environment is vitally important to learning, retention, and recall. In formal training situations, instructors should take measures to ensure that the learning environment affords participants every opportunity to learn. The instructor's role is not to train his/her students but to facilitate his/her students' learning. This can be done most effectively by first creating a proper learning environment in which participants' potential for learning may be enhanced.

The learning environment is to provide:
- A relaxed yet alert atmosphere
- A study area that complies with the four basic learning styles
- An opportunity for participants to distance themselves from stressors associated with their work and/or personal lives that may hamper learning (ie, transition time)

General Information for Instructors
Instructors should follow the basic guidelines in creating stress-free learning environments and study aids for their training program participants.

Development of Study Aids
Instructors are advised to learn as much about their students as possible prior to training sessions in order to identify participants' various learning styles and to plan lessons and activities that complement them.

Additionally, instructors should follow the guidelines for developing handouts when creating study aids (see Section #24 and Appendix C), making sure that the information is presented according to the principles of imagery, the left-right note-study system, and mind-mapping (see Section 11).

All materials must be legible.

Preparation of the Learning Environment

Instructors should prepare their classrooms in advance of training sessions so the room itself sends subliminal messages that indicate the instructor's organization, knowledge of both subject content and training methodology, and readiness and willingness to help. Elements of a learning environment that provide such subliminal information include:

- Relaxation music playing in the background
- Posters of learning affirmations, lettered in blue, that are displayed:
  - At the room's entrance
  - Over the coffee urn
  - On the walls
  - On an overhead projector transparency screen
- A poster that lists learning objectives
- Multicolored peripherals
- A table of resource materials
- Visual media to be used during presentations (these should be within sight and access)
- At each desk or chair:
  - Sets of handouts
  - Sets of the narrative dialogue handout, the front cover of which should include:
    - A brief explanation of the training session

- A comment that most lecture notes are already contained in the handout (this frees the participant to listen to and interact with the material)

Such a setting appeals and sends subliminal messages to both left-brain learners, who require that the learning process be structured and organized, and right-brain learners, who require that creativity be built into the training process and who relate especially to imagery and music.

Introductory Remarks

Instructors may wish to use subliminal tapes as a part of their training methods. If subliminals are used, instructors must:

- Develop and distribute permission forms (see Appendix D) prior to use
- Explain the purpose of:
  - Subliminal tapes
  - Permission forms
- Provide a question-and-answer period before collecting the signed forms

Subliminal tapes must not be played unless all participants have granted permission (see Section #14).

Instructors desiring to use music as a part of training procedures should explain the purpose of the background music and how its use enhances learning. (See Section #15 and Appendices E and F for guidelines for the most effective use of music.)

Also to be explained are the purposes of the peripherals (see Section #12) and learning affirmations (see Section #13) as well as the learning objectives and other visual aids posted throughout the classroom.

At this point of the proceedings, the instructor

should introduce himself/herself and offer his/her qualifications for teaching the program in order to instill in the participants a trust and confidence in their learning facilitator.

If participants are unfamiliar with each other, time should be allowed for individuals to introduce themselves and tell something about their personal interests and why they have chosen this training program. Large classes may be divided into smaller groups for the introduction period. Such an "ice-breaker" serves to remove fears that might otherwise hamper learners' participation in later class discussions. Additionally, because each individual brings to any given situation a unique variety of experiences, such a sharing of experiences enlarges the body of knowledge that the class can use as its "starting point."

The instructor also benefits from the introduction period. His image is enhanced by this activity because participants sense his interest in them (participants' attitudes toward learning are more positive and actual learning is increased when they sense the instructor's interest in them), and the introductions provide him/her with knowledge about the class that can be incorporated into lessons and teaching techniques throughout the training program.

If classes are divided into small groups for introductions, the instructor might use the "ball toss" exercise (Table 22.1) to aid in the process (the exercise should be accompanied by upbeat music). In this exercise, person A holds a sponge ball while introducing himself. When he finishes his introduction, he tosses the ball to any other person in the group; this person, person B, must paraphrase person A, introduce himself, and toss

TABLE 22.1 – **Introduction Exercise: Ball Toss**

1. Person [A] introduces himself:
   - Name
   - Position/work
   - Reason attending training session
   - Hobbies/interests
   - One behavior and/or trait that he/she likes about him/herself

2. Person [A] tosses ball to Person [B].

3. [B] repeats [A]'s name and paraphrases [A]'s introduction.

4. [A] confirms [B]'s paraphrase. If [B] has not repeated [A]'s information correctly, [A] repeats the introduction and [B] responds until [A] is satisfied that the paraphrase is correct.

5. [B] introduces himself, etc.

Source: "Suggestopedia Instructor Training" June, 1982; sponsored by Lozanov Learning Institute (Columbia, MD)

the ball to another. The activity continues until everyone has introduced himself and someone else.

This exercise is intended to suggest supraliminally (see Section #14) that learning is fun — a reminder of pedagogical learning (see Section #2).

Setting Ground Rules

Once introductory remarks and introductions are completed, instructors should establish the ground rules of the training session:

- Participants are encouraged to ask questions and are to be assured that no question is considered "stupid"
- As adults, both facilitators and participants bring their own experiences, resources, and perceptions into the new learning experience. Thus, both facilitators and all participants are "experts". This attitude helps prevent the attitude that the presenter (facilitator) is "above" the participants
- Participants must tell instructors of any difficulties in understanding presented material so that instructors have the opportunity to clarify points in question
- Instructors are to create environments that are conducive to learning
- Participants are to take responsibility for their own learning

By establishing these ground rules, participants should feel welcomed into a positive, stress-free environment for enhanced learning.

References: 43

#23 Relaxation Exercises

Once the proper learning environment has been created, instructors should instigate relaxation before beginning any study session.

Purpose

Instructors should explain the positive effects of relaxation on participants' learning as well as their well-being (see Section #16). Relaxation exercises are intended to:
- Create a relaxed yet alert state in participants
- Provide time for participants to distance themselves from work and/or personal stressors before beginning study
- Provide an opportunity for participants to:
  - Experience the relaxation response that is usually evoked from relaxation exercises
  - Accrue the benefits associated with the relaxation response

Implementation

Any of the relaxation methods (see Section #16) and/or exercises (see Section #18) may be used for this exercise. Step-by-step instructions for various relaxation exercises and breathing techniques are provided in Section #18. (see References 7, 8, and 14 for additional information, exercises, and instructional techniques.)

Instructors should be completely comfortable with the relaxation exercises they present and have the knowledge and skills required for their implementation prior to using them in training sessions. Left-brain learners will want to know of the structure, safety, and security of the exercises proposed, while right-brain learners will want to experience the exercises fully. Thus, instructors must be aware of participants' particular needs and gear their implementation of relaxation exercises accordingly.

It is recommended that each subsequent training session begin with relaxation exercises and that, at the very least, physical stretching exercises (and possibly breathing exercises) be interspersed during day-long training sessions after any pauses or breaks (lunch, etc.)

References: 7, 8, 14, 43

#24 Orchestrated Learning:
Active and Passive

Purposes

See "Participant Advantages" and "Instructor Advantages", below.

Active Learning/Narrative Dialogue
Instructional Methods

Rather than verbally lecturing to an audience, the instructor substitutes an active learning narrative dialogue. This can be done for any subject content and follows the guidelines found below and in Appendix C. Appendix G serves as a beginning role model — an illustrative example. Of course, development of such dialogue is completed prior to the actual start of class.

Immediately following the conclusion of the relaxation exercises (Section 23), the participants are instructed to turn to their dialogue.

They are told that this narrative takes the place of a formal lecture. They, the participants, are instructed to read this to themselves at their own pace. Their handouts contain supplemental information pertinent to the narrative dialogue. Appropriate pages within the narrative shall instruct them where to find the needed information.

During the reading, their instructor, given their permission, shall be playing a subliminal music tape to assist them in their learning. Given permission from everyone, appropriate background music shall be playing in the background. Upon conclusion, they may feel free to leave the room, attending to any needed business, but return by [time]. They may also choose to scan any additional resource material provided by the instructor pertinent to the session's goals and objectives. They may also utilize the free time to practice relaxation breathing or to copy material and information found on the peripherals.

The instructor then reads over the outline contained within an active learning narrative dialogue (see Appendix G, for an example) pronouncing terms participants may not be familiar with. The instructor also emphasized particular components, terms, etc., that shall be important for them to know and in which they shall have subsequent skill development.

Upon everyone's completion of the reading, a general pause of approximately 15 minutes is taken.

Advantages for the Instructor

One of the great advantages of the active learning method of the narrative dialogue is that, because participants work independently, the instructor is free to move around the room to assist participants on a one-on-one basis, an effective teaching/learning situation. The method also ensures that all participants have received the same information.

Another advantage to the instructor is that, if participants do not need his assistance, he/she may use the reading time to:

- Organize his notes for subsequent activities
- Create graphics
- "Catch his/her breath"
- Observe participants to gain knowledge of their learning styles in order to gear subsequent activities accordingly
- Relax and conserve energy for subsequent training activities

Additionally, because the narrative dialogue requires less class time than traditional lecture of the same amount of material, the time saved offers instructors a variety of lesson planning options (see Section #4).

Advantages to Participants

Because study notes are provided in the handouts they receive, participants need not be concerned with taking notes and are thus free to expend their energies in absorbing rather than taking down the information at hand. Also, because the narrative dialogue method is intended to be performed at the participant's own pace, he/she is free to pause whenever he feels the need, to read additional resource material, or to simply sit back and relax. Such freedom allows participants to maintain their adult status during training sessions rather than being made to feel inferior or child-like.

This arrangement also provides participants opportunities to request private one-on-one assistance whenever they feel the need for it — an advantage for learning, since questions can be answered when participants need to have them answered for complete understanding of the material; and an advantage for participants who, because of fear of requesting help while in front of a class, feel freer to ask questions in this more private setting.

The narrative dialogue method appears to be particularly conducive to learning for older adult learners (see Section #27) who appreciate being allowed to work at their own pace and walk around the room to get a closer look at posters of peripherals (see Section 12), learning affirmations (see Section 13), etc.

Guidelines for Development

Regardless of the subject content of an active study narrative dialogue, a few guidelines must be followed if the dialogue is to be effective:

- One narrative is to be created for each unit or module of material to be covered
- Once a component is covered in a dialogue, that component need not be incorporated into the remainder of the unit until review and reinforcement are instituted
- Each dialogue is to contain a traditional overview/outline of the material contained within it; this is especially useful for the left-brain learner who must have structure incorporated into his learning efforts
- The dialogue is to be written in a conversational style
- The format of the dialogue is to follow format guidelines (see Appendix C) and incorporate the left-right note-study system (see Section #11), with the left side of the dialogue page left blank so that participants may create their own associative imagery for each study component
- Supraliminals (see Section #14) are to be incorporated into the dialogue so that participants read such phrases as "I am learning" and "I understand" for themselves; these aid reinforcement and create in participants positive expectations (especially when used simultaneously with subliminal tapes and posted peripherals, learning affirmations, etc.)
- The dialogue is to be written with respect to the learner as an adult (see Section #2) and as a person who brings a myriad of experiences to the learning situation rather than

as a "blank slate" waiting to be filled with information

Passive Learning
Instructional Methods

Once participants have returned from their 15-minute pause after the active learning phase of the training session, the instructor is to explain that passive learning is to begin. He/she is to ask participants to take one or two deep (abdominal) breaths, close their eyes, and imagine their relaxation sanctuaries (see Section #18).

Next, the instructor is to read a summary of the material (dialogue) presented during the active learning session. Participants are to keep their eyes closed and relax as the instructor reads the summary.

The instructor is encouraged to play appropriate background music (classical music with slow tempos [see Appendix E]) during his/her reading of the summary, and he/she should read in cadence with the music, pausing and varying his/her intonation appropriately (see Section #20).

Advantages/Purposes

The passive learning session helps to maintain the relaxed yet alert state of the participants and the stress-free learning environment while reinforcing key subject content.

This method is similar to that of the participant creating an audiocassette tape (in his/her own voice) of key information and playing it back to himself/herself for passive learning (see Section #20).

References: 43

NOTES

#25 Elaboration and Reinforcement

After participants have worked through active and passive learning, the material to be learned must be reviewed and reinforced if it is to be retained for subsequent recall.

Suggested instructional methods for review and reinforcement include:
- Lecture with visual aids
- Left-right note-study system
- Discussion
- Question and answer
- "Ball toss" review
- Other games and competitions

Lecture periods are most effective when they are kept short and are supplemented with visual aids.

Also helpful to the enhancement of participants' learning is a time set aside for their implementation of the left-right note-study system. This activity is especially effective after a break from the active and passive learning sessions and should be immediately preceded by physical stretching and relaxation exercises.

Discussion and question and answer sessions are always helpful to participants, since a discussion period provides an opportunity for clarifications of misunderstood material and since questions that participants may have but are fearful of asking are likely to be asked by another participant.

Question and answer periods are especially effective when used in a game format. The "ball toss" game used for introductions (see Section #22) can be adapted to a question and answer game in which small groups (teams) compete with one another. The instructor tosses a ball into a team and asks a question of whoever catches the ball. If the person answers the question correctly, the team earns one point, and the ball is tossed back to the instructor. If the person cannot answer the question or answers incorrectly, he or she tosses the ball to the opposing team, and whoever catches the ball must answer the question. The team with the highest score wins.

Regardless of the methods used for review and reinforcement, upbeat background music should be played during these activities (see Appendices E and F for appropriate selections.)

Advantages/Purposes

Instructors are encouraged to use these or games of their own creation as tools for review and reinforcement of study material. Games foster the attitude that learning is fun; just the presence of a ball (for the "ball toss" game), for example, evokes the subliminal message that learning can be play.

Elaboration (review) and reinforcement of study material provides participants opportunities to address misunderstandings of any of the material and instructors opportunities to elaborate on the material and supply additional or updated information.

Additionally, if games are used correctly, they provide for the needs of both right- and left-brain learners; right-brain learners are given a chance to experience the learning, and left-brain learners are provided a structured framework for the learning games.

References: 43

#26 Experiential Learning

Experiential learning is a highly effective means of reinforcing study material and newly-acquired skills. The author notes that instructors often feel more comfortable with this component of the accelerated learning training process than any other, probably because the skills that are being reinforced for participants have become "second nature" to instructors at this stage of their careers.

Instructional Methods

Many experiential training methods can be used to reinforce learning. Some of the more common methods include:

- Role playing
- Case studies
- Demonstrations and return demonstrations of learned skills
- Game simulations
- Post-training on-the-job assignments that are monitored by the instructor or the participant's supervisor

Advantages/Purposes

Experiential learning sessions provide a playful and relaxed yet structured learning environment for training program participants. This atmosphere appeals to both right- and left-brain learners.

This component of the learning process also provides participants a transition point, which enhances the likelihood that they will transfer their newly-acquired knowledge and skills to the workplace. It forces participants to activate (ie, actively recall and apply) the learned material, a reinforcement process that enhances retention and increases the chances that the in-class applications will carry over to on-the-job utilization.

Guidelines

Regardless of the specific methods used for experiential learning sessions, a few critical guidelines must be followed:

- The experiential method used must match the learning styles of participants (see Section #10)
- The experiential method used must be structured and emotionally comfortable for participants; for example, two left-brain learners would feel anxious and insecure if asked to role-play in front of an entire class and would result not only in an uncomfortable situation for all concerned but in a waste of training time
- The experiential learning task must relate to:
  - The learning objectives established for that training session
  - The study material to be reinforced
  - The newly-acquired skills
  - The knowledge and skills that participants must acquire in order to perform their respective jobs
- The experiential learning task must be used *ONLY* as a learning tool and *NEVER* as a means of play alone
- The experiential method must not disrupt the relaxed yet alert state already created in the participants and learning environment; this means that instructors must incorpo-

rate as many accelerated learning techniques (see Sections #10 through #16) as possible into the experiential learning session, including playing background music (see Appendices E and F for appropriate selections)

Resources

Professional training associations (local chapters, if available) offer training skills for instructors. Recommended organizations include:

1. American Society for Training and Development
    1630 Duke Street
    Alexandria, VA 22313
    703/683-8100
2. Hospitals and Health Industry Group Network, a subdivision of American Society for Training and Development
3. American Society for Health Care Education and Training
    A division of the American Hospital Association (AHA)
    840 North Lake Shore Drive
    Chicago, IL 60611
    312/280-6000
    This organization focuses on training for health care educators.
4. Section #35 — For sources of general accelerated learning methodology training

References: 43

NOTES

#27 Special Needs of the Older Adult Learner

Overview

America's population is aging. For the past 20 years, the population rate of Americans aged 65 and over has doubled compared to the increase rate of other Americans, due, for the most part, to medical advances that increase the life span. Additionally, an awareness of preventive medicine (such as wellness programs in nutrition, physical fitness, stress management, relaxation therapy, public non-smoking campaigns, etc.) has motivated many to become responsible for their own health.

The result of these factors is that greater numbers of people are remaining active for longer periods of time than ever before. Women, for example, after having raised their children and because they are remaining healthy into their later years, are returning to or are starting careers. Consequently, the fields of education and training increasingly find the older worker returning to the campus and/or filling seats in organization-sponsored formal training programs.

This segment of society is also receiving an education from health care professionals in terms of following instructions for medications, specialized diets, therapy, etc. As institutional health costs rise, more treatments are performed in the home, a situation that requires training for caregivers. As institutional health becomes more technical and complex, so too, will home health care; again, caregivers will be called upon to increase their knowledge and skills.

Therapists and caregivers cannot assume that once a patient has been given a sheet of instructions (often accompanied unfortunately cursory explanation), the patient can carry out the perscribed treatment. As noted previously, much of learning is lost within 24 hours of its presentation unless reinforced (see Section 20).

The literature on education and training, whether from the traditional or accelerated learning methodologies, does not mention the needs of older adult learners (defined as those ages 55 and older) or the implications of those needs for training and education.

The following is an attempt to address the means by which these learners can be helped, suggesting applications of specific accelerated learning methods that may help penetrate the learning barriers that result from the natural aging process.

Research Findings

The findings presented have implications for the health care practitioner, counselor, educator, and trainer.

Physiological Functioning

Research studies are conclusive in their findings: as aging occurs, individuals experience declines in:
- Depth perception functioning
- Vision
- Hearing
- Psychomotor response and reaction times

Depth Perception Functioning

Depth perception functions rapidly begin to deteriorate between the ages of 40 and 50.

Vision
The decline in vision generally begins at age 45 for Caucasians and age 40 for non-Caucasians.

Light
One test indicates that only one-third as much white light is perceived by a 60-year-old as by a 20-year-old, and the eyes of an older adult require a longer period of time to adjust to rapid and/or extreme changes in lighting.

Perception
When presented with ambiguous figures, older adults are more likely to retain their original perceptions of such entities than younger people. Their visual perception judgment is less flexible and, thus, these individuals tend to have greater difficulty extracting specific information from a complex visual configuration.

Perception Masking
Perception masking is the phenomenon that occurs when the second of two visual stimuli, presented in quick succession, blurs or erases the perception of the first. Older adults require a longer period of time to recover from the first stimulus; thus, this phenomenon is common in older adults. It is possible that older adults are incapable and, thus, unwilling to proceed to new tasks until recovery has occurred—a situation that may impact psychomotor response and reaction times (see below).

Color Discrimination/Glare
The ability to discriminate among subtleties of colors (eg, blue-green) decreases with age, as

does the ability to tolerate and recover from glare (see Section #12); recovery from glare requires nine seconds for a 65-year-old as opposed to two seconds for a 15-year-old.

Hearing

Regarding auditory decline, older adults experience:
- Decreased awareness of high-pitched sounds (pitch: high or low sound frequencies)
- Decreased sensitivity to pure tones
- Difficulty distinguishing low-pitched sounds
- Bilateral hearing loss
- More hearing loss associated with high frequencies
- Restricted functional range of speech intensitiy (An older person can't talk as loudly as a younger person)
- Difficulty filtering out background noise

Psychomotor Response and Reaction Times

Research data overwhelmingly demonstrates that such psychomotor responses as automobile driving skills and handwriting slowly decline with age. Response time differences are not discernable until approximately age 40, after which the decline becomes an important factor in explaining individual performance levels.

Organization and Assimilation of New Information

Older adults often have difficulty organizing new information. As individuals age, they incorporate more and more learning (knowledge, skills, values) and experiences into their brain's "storage banks"; thus, there is a greater amount of stored information with which new material must be connected, related, and compared (see Section #6). For the older adult who is attempting to learn new material, the process of search-recall-recognize requires more time simply because of the abundance of stored material that must be accessed and responded to.

However, because of the increased amount of stored information, older adult learners have greater capacities than their younger counterparts to:
- Interrelate new material with previous learning
- Cognitively create concepts
- Make fine distinctions among abstract concepts
- Predict outcomes of alternative actions (i.e, they possess introspective wisdom)

Neurological impairments notwithstanding, these abilities do not decline until older adults reach advanced ages, if then.

Memory Loss

Older adults experience greater decline in short- than long-term memory (see Section #6). Memory loss seems to be related to:
- The meaningfulness of the material learned (see Section #3)
- Lack of reinforcement and application of the material (see Section #20)
- Interference: the overload of short-term memory with too much stimuli; often, anxiety is a contributing factor (see Section 16).

Motivational Considerations

Several studies have concluded that higher scores in tests measuring for dogma are attained with increasing age. Additionally, a strong correlation exists between increasing age in rigidity of thought.

Older adults also approach the learning of new material and risk-taking with caution. Their barriers to risk-taking have been identified as:

- Alienation
- Hopelessness
- Defensiveness

Implications for Training and Education

The following recommendations for instructional methods and techniques for the enhancement of learning for older adults are designed for the formal training environment, though they are also relevant to one-on-one training, counseling, coaching, and other educational settings.

Compensations for Vision Deficiencies

Instructors are urged to consider the vision difficulties of older learners when preparing classrooms and visual aids. In particular, instructors should:

- Ensure adequate lighting in the classroom
- Arrange visual aids in such a way as to avoid glare
- Avoid abrupt lighting changes, as occur before and after film presentations. If dimmer switches are available, use them; if not, pause before continuing class
- Use strongly contrasting colors for color-coded material
- Use LARGE PRINT whenever possible
- Avoid presentations of complex charts. If possible, divide the information into several components and present on separate charts; if this is not feasible, present the chart as an

overview and discuss its components separately
- Do not turn the overhead projector on and off
- Allow extra time between presentations of transparencies; if transparencies must be presented quickly, provide duplicates of the information in the forms of peripheral visual aids or handouts
- Avoid flip charts; instead, mount separate charts on a wall or provide the information as handouts or peripheral visual aids

Compensations for Hearing Deficiencies

Instructors should consider participants' auditory deficiencies when presenting information, remembering to:
- Speak slowly and clearly
- Face the class when speaking (rather than speaking to a chart or transparency)
- Eliminate background noise (eg, the fan of an overhead projector)
- Recommend that hearing-impaired participants sit near the instructor

Compensations for Psychomotor Response and Reaction Time Deficiencies

Instructors should allow additional time for older learners to complete psychomotor tasks, due to their slowed response times. Older learners' need for extra time allowances is one reason that self-pacing is a particularly effective and advantageous learning tool.

Accelerated Learning and Older Learners

The methods and principles of accelerated learning also are advantageous to older learners.

The following is a list of the accelerated learning methods and principles that address specific needs of older learners:
- Need for self-pacing:
  - Narrative dialogue:
    - Active orchestrated learning; learners read at their own pace
    - Passive orchestrated learning; because the instructor must synchronize his reading with the slow tempo of classical music, he is forced into a slow delivery of the material
  - Imagery
  - Music
  - Peripheral visual aids
  - Relaxation exercises
- Visual deficiencies:
  - Imagery, ie, the integration of all senses on the conscious, paraconscious, and subconscious levels
  - Review and reinforcement, especially passive learning
  - Passive orchestrated learning
- Perception masking:
  - Peripheral visual aids
- Hearing deficiencies:
  - Narrative dialogue, ie, active orchestrated learning
- Psychomotor response and reaction time deficiencies:
  (See Need for self-pacing, above)
- Organization and assimilation of new information:
  - Peripheral visual aids
  - Music (to attain an alpha brain wave state)
  - Relaxation exercises (to attain an alpha brain wave state)

- Learning styles
- Subliminals (auditory)
- Memory loss:
  - Peripheral visual aids
  - Music
  - Relaxation exercises
  - Imagery
  - Learning styles
  - Subliminals (visual and auditory)
  - Learning affirmations
  - Creation of a stress-free learning environment
  - Active study
  - Review and reinforcement
  - All other components of the accelerated learning training model
- Motivation and risk-taking:
  - Subliminals (auditory)
  - Learning affirmations
  - Peripheral visual aids
  - Learning styles
  - Creation and maintenance of a stress-free learning environment

References: 2, 28

Resources: For further research information on the older adult learner, relating to cognitive development and the implications for education and training, contact:

K. Warner Schaie, Ph.D.
Sherry Willis, Ph.D.
  Penn State Univ. Gerontology Center
  S-210 Henderson
  Human Development Building
  University Park, PA 16802
  (814/865-1710)

NOTES

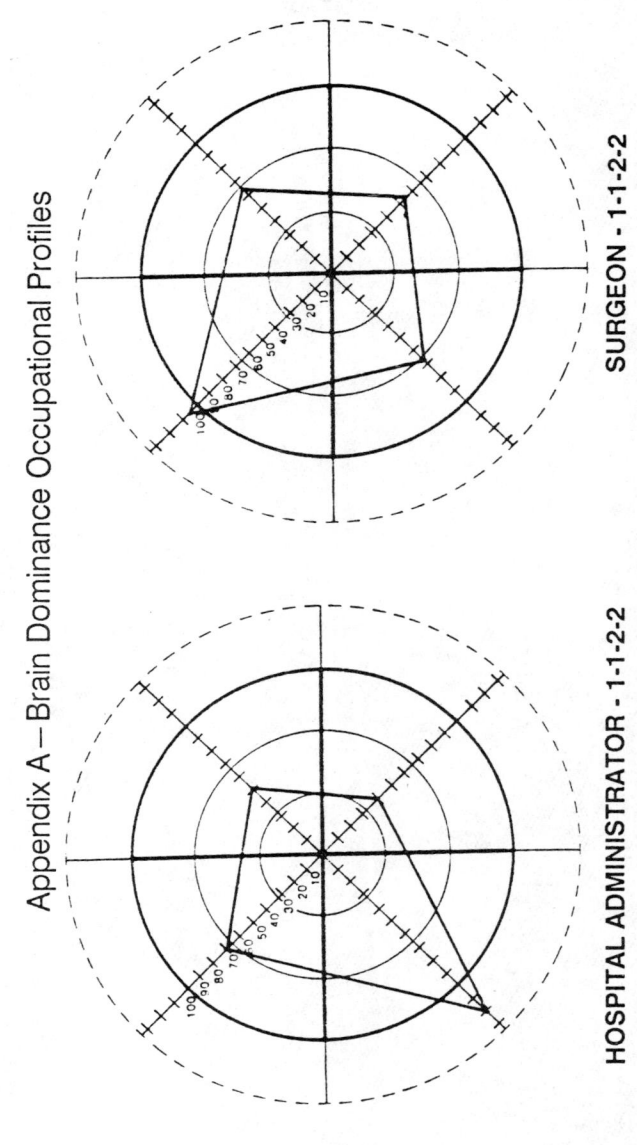

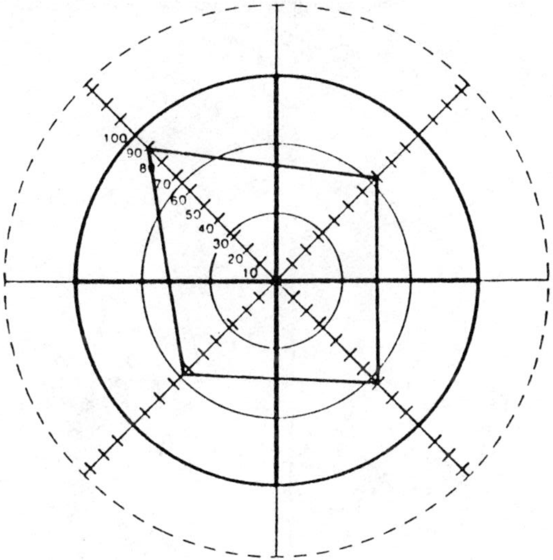

GENERAL PRACTITIONER - 1-2-1-1

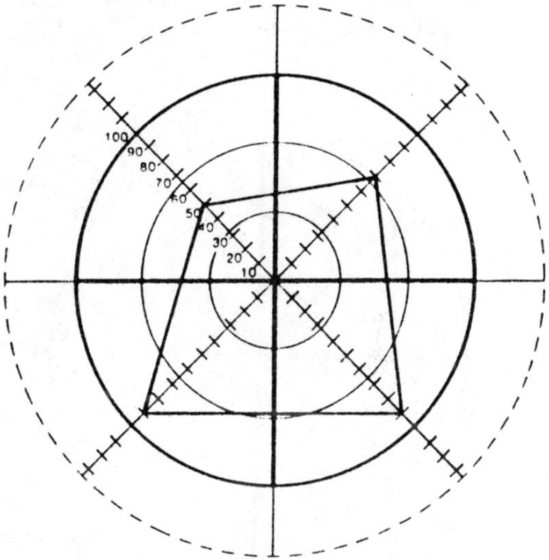

SUPERVISORY NURSE - 2-1-1-1

28.

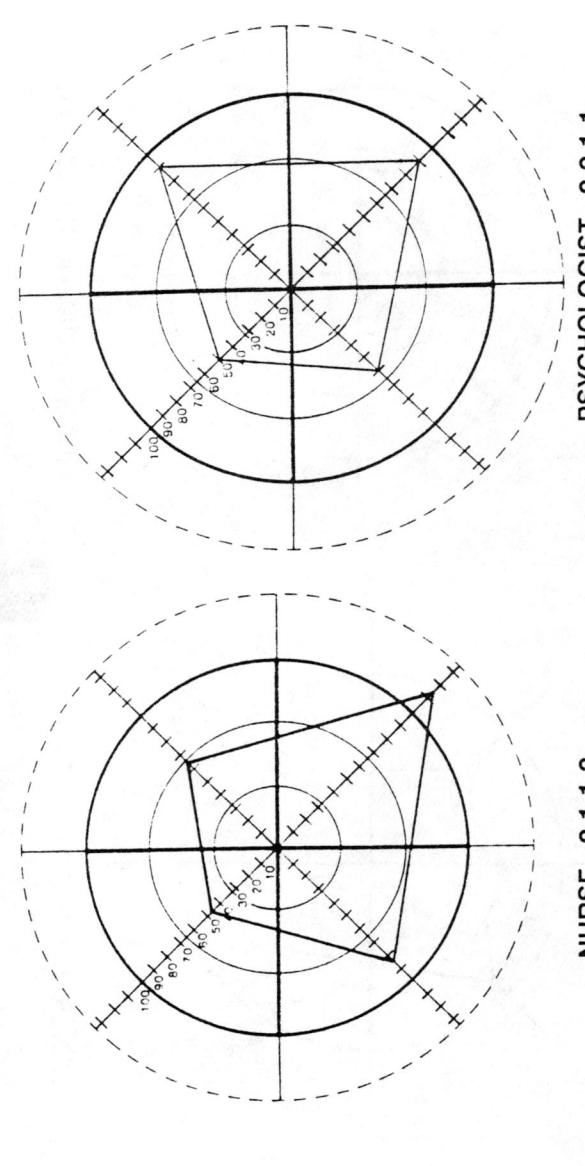

NURSE - 2-1-1-2

PSYCHOLOGIST - 2-2-1-1

Herrmann N: The Creative Brain. Lake Lure, NC: Brain Books, 1988. Reprinted with permission by the Ned Herrmann Group, Applied Creative Services, Ltd.

NOTES

Appendix B — Brain Dominance Occupational Profiles: Narrative Descriptions

The following narrative descriptions correspond to the schematic occupational brain dominance profiles in Appendix A.

1-1-2-2: Hospital Administrator and Surgeon

This is a double dominant profile with primaries in the Left mode — Upper Left A and Lower Left B quadrants. It is the second most common profile in the general population, representing 15 percent, and the most common profile for males, representing 21 percent. The profile is characterized by a logical, analytic, technical orientation, and is effective in rational problem solving from the Upper Left A quadrant. Lower Left B quadrant preferences include planning, organizing, implementing and administrative activities. In this profile, the processing modes of Upper Left A and Lower Left B would clearly be the most preferred, and the interpersonal, emotional, and spiritual modes of Lower Right C and the holistic, creative, and synthesizing modes of Upper Right D would be at the secondary level, yet functional. This profile is typical of those occupations in technical fields, such as engineering and manufacturing, financial positions, middle managers, and in general, those positions for which left mode processing is clearly most important, and the right mode processing being necessary, yet secondary.

1-2-1-1: General Practitioner

This profile is triple dominant, with three preferred quadrants. These primaries occur in Upper

Left A, Lower Right C, and Upper Right D quadrants. This is a multi-dominant profile that would be characterized by well balanced processing modes of Upper Left A — the analytic, logical, and rational processing; the interpersonal, emotional, and intuitive thinking modes of Lower Right C, combined with the artistic, creative, and holistic processing modes of the Upper Right D quadrant. The Lower Left B secondary quadrant would be functional, yet clearly of less preference in terms of organizing, control, structure and conservative thinking styles. This profile is also double dominant in the upper modes, both left and right. This individual would be more experimental than safekeeping and more emotional than controlled. Occupations would involve those with less administrative detail and more attention to broad concepts, strategic planning as compared to operational planning, and those occupations tending towards a more "generalized" nature. Positions involving technical innovation and future planning fit this profile along with human resource and development professions.

2-1-1-1: Supervisor Nurse

This is a triple dominant profile with two primaries in the right mode, Lower Right C and Upper Right D quadrants, and the third in Lower left B. It is the most common of all profiles, with 16 percent of the population exhibiting this multi-dominant array of preferences. It is the clear majority for the female population, 24 percent exhibiting this profile. The 2-1-1-1 profile is characterized by its multi-dominant and "generalized" nature, and fairly balanced amount of understanding and ability to use the three primary quadrants — the preferred processing modes being creative and holistic in Upper Right D, interpersonal and feeling in Lower Right C, and planning and organizing in the Lower Left B. The Upper Left quadrant A is least preferred, but still the person is typically quite functional in their use of the logical and analytical aspects of this quadrant. This profile is typical of many personnel and human resource professionals, including teachers as well as those whose occupations require an understanding and ability to function on many levels, such as social workers, executive secretaries, and supervisory nurses.

2-1-1-2: Nurse

This profile is a double dominant profile with the two primaries in the Lower Left B and Lower Right C quadrants. It is a double primary in the lower, visceral area. The profile is characterized by very strong preferences in conservative thinking and controlled behavior with a desire for organization and structure as well as detail and accuracy from the Lower Left B quadrant. Persons with this profile tend to worry about details. The primary in the Lower Right C would equally show itself by emotional and interpersonal preferences, an interest in music, and a sense of spirituality. It would also show in an intuitive "feelings" sense of this person. The two lower primaries could represent an important duality for the person to resolve within themselves. The opposing qualities of control and structure, of "form" — and the emotional and interpersonal "feelings" can cause internal conflict. The clear secondary preferences of the upper modes, both Upper Left A and Upper Right D, are also characteristic of this profile, with logical and analytical in the Upper Left A quadrant and holistic and creative thinking of

Upper Right D quadrant. Occupations typical of those people with this profile include nurses, homemakers, secretaries, and other members of the "helping" profession.

2-2-1-1: Psychologist

This profile features two primaries in the right mode, quadrants C and D, and two secondaries in the left mode, quadrants A and B. It is the third most common profile in the population at large, at 14 percent, and with only a relatively slight difference in the male and female populations — respectively 11 percent and 17 percent. Typical characteristics would include the ability to be creative, holistic, and synthesizing in the Upper Right D quadrant, and interpersonal, emotional, and spiritual in the Lower Right C quadrant. The left mode secondaries with logical, analytical, and mathematical thinking styles from Upper Left A, and the organizational, planning, and structure from Lower Left B, would be functional, yet clearly secondary to the preferred right modes of thinking. Those with this profile often have the occupations of teaching or facilitating. Other occupations include the arts, such as writers, musicians, artists, and designers, as well as those in the "helping" fields — psychologists and counselors. This profile could also support entrepreneurial behavior, since it features the imaginative, innovating, and "risk" oriented behavior of the right mode, quadrants C and D without the control or preference of the structured, logical and conservative modes of the left quadrants A and B.

Herrmann N: *The Creative Brain.* Lake Lure, NC: Brain Books, 1988. Reprinted with permission by the Ned Herrmann Group, Applied Creative Services, Ltd.

Appendix C — Format Guidelines for Creating a Text

The following is a guideline for creating a text that adheres to the principles of accelerated learning methods.

1. Textual elements should be placed as follows:
   - All prose on the right side of a page or right page of a book
   - All artwork (symbols, pictures, charts, graphs, etc.) on the left side of a page or left page of a book
   - Highlighted information (key terms, definitions, concepts, reinforcers, quotes, motivators, affirmations, etc.) on the extreme right side of a page or the right page of a book

This placement follows brain-mind function, ie:

- The right hemisphere deals with visuo-spatial relationships, art, and imagery
- The left hemisphere deals with analytical and logical relationships

Whatever is seen with the left eye, physiologically connected to both the left and right hemispheres, crosses over into the right hemisphere via the brain's corpus callosum. Thus, a natural function of the right hemisphere (imagery) is reinforced when information is presented in this format.

References: 25, 43

2. For the narrative presentation of subject content:
    - Line lengths should be limited to six or seven words
    - Type should be double-spaced
    - Long passages of information should be divided into smaller sections, if possible
    - New or key terms, definitions, concepts, relationships, etc. should be *highlighted*, using different colors and typefaces and/or separating them from the text for **SPECIAL ATTENTION**
    - New or key terms should be typed in LARGE PRINT; the larger the print, the greater the chance for memory retention and recall
    - The typeface for and format of words should follow the connotations and the mental images they inspire; for example, the word "relaxed" should be printed as "relaxed..." rather than "RELAXED!!!"
    - Information should be repeated throughout the text to aid reinforcement. Information should be repeated throughout the text to aid reinforcement
3. White space should be provided throughout the text to provide the reader/participant with space in which to create his own notes, symbols, and images. Blank spaces should be positioned on the left side of the page.

Instructors should allow classroom time for learners to create these notes and images; in addition to reinforcing learning, these periods serve as pauses between presentations of new material.

4. Columns of information presented in charts, graphs, etc. should be separated from one another and/or from the text by space rather

than by bars or lines. Bars clutter the text and place a barrier between related material, whereas open space sends a subliminal message that the material is interrelated.
5. New information should be presented in clusters of seven to nine items each, the number of items short-term memory most effectively retains.
6. Because retention is greater for items presented at the beginning and end of a block of text, the most important items in a cluster of information should be presented first and last.

NOTES

Appendix D — Permission Form: Learning Affirmation Audio Subliminals

TO THE PARTICIPANT: Please read the following.

What is an audio subliminal message? An audio subliminal message is a message that has been embedded into an audiocassette tape of a musical composition and/or of other sounds (such as a tape of environmental sounds) and is designed to be absorbed by the subconscious mind. The conscious mind hears only the music, while the subconscious mind absorbs the specific suggestions of the subliminal messages.

The purpose of using subliminal messages is to increase subconscious acceptance of suggestions. Subliminal messages help to maximize learning in that their proper use corresponds to functions of both right- and left-brain hemispheres.

The effectiveness of subliminal messages depends upon the manner in which they are technically developed and incorporated into an audiocassette tape and upon the receptiveness of the participant; subliminal messages must conform to a participant's value systems if they are to be effective.

The subliminal learning affirmations used in this training program have been developed by R.G. Swartz and Associates, Management Impact Skills, P.O. Box 7568, Lancaster, PA 17604-7568 (717) 299-5061, and the subliminal tape project was coordinated with Accelerated Learning Systems, Inc., Annapolis, MD. A classical pianist assisted with the musical selections. The learning affirmations presented have been in use by Swartz and Associates for several years in training workshops/courses.

NOTE: Subliminal tapes are not intended as substitutes for medical and/or professional treatments but may be used in conjunction with such treatments.

Listed below are the learning affirmations that are subliminally embedded into the audiocassette tapes of music that will be played during this particular training program:

1. I am receptive to learning now.
2. I am absorbing information now.
3. I am utilizing the information for the good of all concerned.

My signature indicates my permission for the instructor to play subliminal learning affirmation tapes. Because audiocassette tapes not containing subliminal messages will also be played during training sessions, I understand that the instructor will announce when a subliminal tape is to be played.

Name _____
(Please Print)

Signature _____

Date _____

Title of course/workshop _____

Appendix E — Musical Learning Notes

1. The three types of music that foster relaxation, reduce stress, and enhance learning and healing are:
   - Classical
   - New Age
   - Environmental sounds. Two recommended series are *Environments* and *Solitudes.* Tempos of environmental records approximate those of *largo* and *andante* movements of classical music and of many New Age selections
2. Music types recommended for use during specific learning situations are:
   - For the introduction of new, unfamiliar subject content:
     - Classical music with *largo* or *andante* movements, especially selections from the Baroque, Neo-classical, Classical, and Romantic periods
     - Subliminal tapes; recommended is the 90-minute *Swartz "Sound Learning".* This tape is also available without subliminal messages from Accelerated Learning Systems, Inc., 6193 Summit Trail, Norcross, GA 30092; 404/446-3852
   - For review of or practice of skills that require knowledge of material:
     - Classical music of any tempo, period, or composer. Recommended are:
       - Symphonies by Boccherini and Haydn
       - *Water Music* by Handel
       - *The Four Seasons* by Vivaldi
       - *Kanon in D* by Pachelbel
       - *The Brandenberg Concertos* by Bach

- Selections by Mozart and Beethoven
- New Age music (see Appendix F), such as:
  - *Side 1: Celestial Soda Pop*, in *Deep Breakfast*, by Ray Lynch
  - *Seascapes* and *After the Rain*, by M. Jones
  - *Silk Road* in *Silk Road*, by Kitaro
- For use during registration time, as participants enter the learning environment, and during breaks from study sessions:
- Up-tempo (*allegro*) classical music
- Jazz music may also be played. Recommended are:
  - *Chase the Clouds Away* and *Can't We Do This All Night Long?* in *Chase the Clouds Away* by Chuck Mangione
  - *Sketches of Spain, Miles at Newport,* and *Basic Miles* by Miles Davis
  - *Take Five, Time Out* by Dave Brubeck
- For relaxation:
  - While creating a sanctuary:
    - New Age music, such as Side 1: *Pacelbel Kanon* of *Timeless Motion* by Daniel Kobialka
  - While performing deep breathing and "22-count" breathing exercises:
    - New Age music, such as *Vivaldi Largo, Dream Passage* by Kobialka, and/or
    - Recordings of environmental sounds:
      - *Ocean Surf in a Hidden Cove*
      - *Solitudes, Vol. 2,* and/or
      - Classical music, and/or
      - Subliminal tapes, such as *Self-Healing, Sound Healing* by Roger Swartz

- After deep breathing exercises, New Age (*Seascapes* or *After the Rain* by M. Jones) or *allegro* classical music
- For physical and physical progressive relaxation, New Age selections, such as:
  - *Ascension to the All That Is* (see Appendix F)
  - Side 1: *Mamma Tierra*, in *Machu Picchu Impressions* by Rusty Crutcher
  - *Sky of Mind* by Ray Lynch
- While developing affirmations and imaging their achievements, New Age music, especially, Side 1: *Pachelbel Kanon* in *Timeless Motion* by Daniel Kobialka

NOTES

Appendix F – New Age Music

	Composer	Company	Selections	Application
1.	Jon Bernoff and Marcus Allen	Dream Weaver Music BMI/Rising Sun Records	*Breathe.* Environmental sounds mixed with instruments, et al	Side 1: Relaxation. Side 2: Up-tempo; uplifting
2.	Jim Chappell	Unspeakable Freedom Productions	*Dusk.* Piano	Contemplation
3.	Rusty Crutcher	Emerald Green Sound Production	*Machu Picchu Impressions.* Environmental sounds mixed with instruments, et al	Associative Meditation Yoga exercises
4.	Alex Jones and Doug Cutler	Alex Jones	*Kali's Dream.* Piano	Peacefulness. Contemplation
5.	Michael Jones	MCA Records	*Seascapes. After the Rain*	Peacefulness. Contemplation
6.	Kitaro	Polygram	*Silk Road*	Up-tempo; uplifting

7.	Daniel Kobialka	Lisem	*Timeless Motion. Dream Passage* Violin plus. It is a whole series. A mix of classical and New Age	Relaxation. Self-motivation
8.	Ray Lynch	Music West	*Deep Breakfast. Sky of Mind.* Synthesizers and natural instruments	*DB:* Up-tempo; uplifting. *SM:* Relaxation, meditation, contemplation
9.	Mike Rowland	Narada	*The Fairy Ring.* Piano and synthesized strings	Contemplation.
10.	Robert Slap	Valley of the Sun	*Ascension to All That Is.* Organ, synthesized instruments, synthesized voices	Associative and non-associative meditation
11.	Upper Astral	Valley of the Sun	*Crystal Cave. (Back to Atlantis).* Harp, synthesizer, chimes, and synthesized voices	Associative Meditation, Massage
12.	George Winston	Windham Hill	*December.* Piano	Contemplation

Appendix G – Active Learning Narrative Dialogue: An Learning Example

An Active Learning Narrative Dialogue
Developed by
R.G. Swartz and Associates

Copyright 1986. R.G. Swartz and Associates, P.O. Box 7568, Lancaster, PA 17604-7568. All rights reserved. No portion of this program shall be utilized, disseminated, and/or electronically stored and retrieved in any manner without prior written permission.

Dialogue I: Accelerated Learning—Outline

I. Brain/Mind Research
   1. The triune brain
      A. Reptilian
      B. Mammalian
      C. Neocortex
   2. Left- and right-brain hemispheric functions
   3. The four brain waves and their characteristics
   4. Limbic system functions
   5. Reticular activating system (RAS) functions
   6. The neuroanatomic brain model—Distributing information
      A. Dendrites and axons
      B. Synapses
   7. The holographic brain/mind interactive model—Processing information
   8. Relationships
      A. The definition and implications of stress
      B. Alpha, learning, stress, and the limbic system
      C. The holographic model to synchronicity, creativity, and patterns of behavior

II. Learning
   1. Andragogy
      A. Definition and four characteristics
      B. Relationship to accelerated learning
   2. Accelerated learning
      A. Definition and eight components
      B. Georgi Lozanov
         1. Suggestology
         2. Supermemory/hypermnesia
      C. Largo movement classical music

D. Relationship of accelerated learning to
   1. Left- and right-brain hemispheric functions
   2. The holographic brain/mind interactive model
   3. Music, the limbic system, and alpha

DIALOGUE I: ACCELERATED LEARNING — BACKGROUND

NOTE: The following is an *excerpt* of the original dialogue. (The subject content of the entire dialogue is outlined on the previous page.) This excerpt is intended to be used as an *example* for those wishing to develop their own active learning narrative dialogues. The active learning narrative dialogue format can be used in the instruction of any subject area and content (see Section #24). An actual dialogue for participants would follow all format guidelines found in Section 24 and Appendix C.

PRESENTER: Good day. I am your presenter today. Some call me a facilitator; others, a mental traffic controller, since we are working with mind power.

PARTICIPANT: You mean brain power, don't you?

PRESENTER: In part. Brain/mind power, if you wish. How about this? A *holographic brain/mind interactive model,* producing brain/mind power.

PARTICIPANT: Wha . . . ? A holographic brain/mind interactive model. What does that mean?

PRESENTER: I prefer the theory that the brain is of the body and the mind is of the self/soul/consciousness, but whatever you wish. An analogy: the mind is the operator of the computer, or brain.

PARTICIPANT: Then the human mind is a computer as well? Please explain.

PRESENTER: The human brain is like a computer, capable of performing many functions simultaneously. The brain, housed in the human skull, has 100 billion-plus cells. Let's call these cells *neurons*. Each neuron has thousands of tiny fibers, called *dendrites* and *axons*, extending from it. These fibers conduct messages across gaps between the neurons, called *synapses*, creating an infinitesimal system of interconnected patterns, memory traces, etc. The possibilities are endless.

PARTICIPANT: Is this what is meant by the statement that we utilize only 10 to 15 percent of our potential?

PRESENTER: I'm not even sure we utilize that much. Given current research findings, I contend that it's more like five percent, or even less.

PARTICIPANT: Like what findings?

PRESENTER: Whew! A tall order.

PARTICIPANT: Try me. I'm very curious about this stuff.

PRESENTER: Let me summarize what is important for learning. I call it ACCELERATED LEARNING.

PARTICIPANT: What's that?

PRESENTER: Let me back up and introduce it by way of your first question regarding brain/mind research findings. First of all, the human brain has been found evolutionarily to be *three-fold*. This triune brain is composed of:
- The reptilian brain, the oldest
- The paleomammalian or mammalian brain
- The neomammalian, neocortex, or human brain, the most recent

Each component is superimposed over its evolutionarily earlier counterpart in a pattern of brain-within-brains.

PARTICIPANT: Three. OK, I've got that.

PRESENTER: The reptilian brain is positioned at the top of the brain stem. It contains the *reticular activating system*, referred to as the RAS, which is the brain's alarm bell. Without this alarm system, human beings would be comatose. The RAS:
- Sends impulses to the cortex by traveling up the sensory nerve column
- Amplifies and excites sensory and motor impulses
- Inhibits effects which reduce and calm sensory and motor impulses

The mammalian brain was next in the evolutionary process. Positioned over the reptilian brain, the mammalian brain is situated deep within the valley of the neocortex, the area of the brain that contains the left and right hemispheres. The mammalian brain also houses another important system, LIMBIC SYSTEM, which is concerned with:
- ATTENTION
- LEARNING
- EMOTION
- MEMORY

It mediates messages received from the outer environment on their way to the neocortex and maintains an equilibrium of mood and emotion. The limbic system can be described physically as rings curled around the reptilian brain; limbic, in Greek, means "bordering around."

PARTICIPANT: Are you implying that a state of balance—calm or relaxed, if you will—has an impact on learning?

PRESENTER: I was coming to that. Yes! Precisely! Very good! Over the limbic system lies a "rug" of gray matter, the neocortex or thinking cap. The neocortex is divided into two *brain hemispheres*, the *left and the right*, each possessing specialized functions. Take out your chart and review it.

Directions:	Turn to Brain Hemisphere charts/handouts. After review, continue reading this dialogue.

PRESENTER: Do you have any questions?

PARTICIPANT: No. The information seems clear. I am learning quite a bit.
Wait. I do have one question. Do these hemispheric functions relate to how the brain *processes* information?

PRESENTER: Correct! You got it! Any other questions?

PARTICIPANT: Yes. There are three brains. How does the limbic system aid learning and information processing?

PRESENTER: When the limbic system is in balance, an individual experiences less stress; and the lower the stress, the greater the potential for learning and for overall physical and mental functioning.

PARTICIPANT: What is stress?

PRESENTER: I define it this way:
Stress is the positive or negative physiological response/end result within the body that is created by physical and/or mental stimuli (of the external and/or internal environment) that interact with the emotions.
When either brain hemisphere is in a state of relaxation, it emits a brain wave pattern known as *ALPHA*. There are four brain waves. Look at your next handout.

> **Directions:** Review the Brain Waves handout. When finished, continue reading narrative dialogue.

PARTICIPANT: Let's go over brain waves some more, particularly the practical significance of each.

PRESENTER: Certainly. To begin, the *BETA* brain wave pattern is the frequency through which input from your conscious senses is received. By conscious, I mean not only the typical five senses but also the sense of motion. Beta brain waves keep us grounded in the physical world.

PARTICIPANT: Then this is the most important brain wave, right?

PRESENTER: No, not really. Each brain wave type is important, and each has its strengths and weaknesses.

PARTICIPANT: What are beta's strengths and weaknesses?

PRESENTER: The beta brain wave is the conscious mind's coping frequency. Without it, a person could not function in our modern, complex world. But, remember, beta is also the frequency of stress, anxiety, apprehension, and competition.

PARTICIPANT: But isn't that good for me? To keep me attuned? Sharp?

PRESENTER: Not if the stress is constant. During long, intensive periods of stress the heart beats faster, blood pressure rises, and the digestive system slows. These are indications, incidentally, that diet and nutrition require careful attention when a person is engaged in stressful activities/situations that can cause blood sugar to increase and the immune system to deteriorate and eventually break down. Such conditions can lead to disease — it's no accident that the word "disease" breaks down into "dis-ease."

This is why the limbic system is so important. It balances our:
- Emotions
- Responses to emotions
- Acts and actions
- Thoughts that influence emotions
- Stress levels

PARTICIPANT: I see. This gets us back to the definition of stress. Then, going back to alpha, is it better? Is *theta*?

PRESENTER: Alpha and theta brain waves are conducive to relaxation. The beauty of alpha is that, while it is slower than beta, it provides full awareness, a relaxed yet alert state of mind. This awareness can be focused for concentration — a person can be actively engaged in a project while remaining calm and self-centered; this, by the way, is the true meaning of self-centeredness. Alpha is, thus, a frequency conducive to creation and beneficial to learning, retention, and recall.

PARTICIPANT: The implications for accessing alpha for fulfilling potential or living up to capabilities are becoming apparent.

PRESENTER: I concur 100 percent. And alpha is a great frequency for self-motivation, self-conditioning, problem-solving, and healing.

PARTICIPANT: You said that alpha is beneficial for learning, retention, and recall. Explain further.

PRESENTER: Look at your brain wave chart.

Directions:	Follow along the chart while continuing to read the narrative dialogue

PRESENTER: Do you participate in any water sports?

PARTICIPANT: I used to white water raft, and I like to canoe.

PRESENTER: OK. Let's use the analogy of brain waves to water action. What happens when you throw a rock into a fast moving body of water? Any ripple effect?

PARTICIPANT: No. The water dissipates rather than ripples.

PRESENTER: Take a look at beta. Is it a fast or slow brain wave?

PARTICIPANT: Fast. Little or no ripple effect here with the rock.

PRESENTER: How about alpha?

PARTICIPANT: Slower. More ripple effect.

PRESENTER: And what is the relationship to learning?

PARTICIPANT: The rock is a bit of information! The slower the brain wave, the greater the impact of the information, or rock.

PRESENTER: Yes! The ripple is the patterning. New information has a greater opportunity of being encoded into the brain's memory cells when the pattern is "slow" and the brain "printout" shows large moving brain waves.

Therefore, initial learning, retention, and long-term recall are enhanced because the slow frequency allows time for the information to be encoded. Also, for real learning, new information must be encoded deeply within those large, slow patterns, much like a rut is deepened every time a wheel drives in it.

PARTICIPANT: Hence the need for reinforcement.

PRESENTER: Precisely! But we can't reinforce something that hasn't been encoded. Sometimes we try to reinforce learning based on an erroneous assumption that initial learning has taken place. Learning must have occurred before it can be reinforced.

PARTICIPANT: Is this where the *theta* brain wave comes in? How does theta affect learning?

PRESENTER: I call the *theta* brain wave "super alpha." Gurus, yogis, shamans, and healers all function at this frequency, a state in which the functions associated with alpha are enlarged and expanded. The theta pattern is difficult to sustain, however, unless control over the brain wave frequencies has been mastered.

Because the theta frequency is so slow and low on the registry of the four (4) brainwaves, it is easy to drop into the deep sleep of the *delta* frequency when attempting to sustain it.

PARTICIPANT: Are we in delta when we dream? Is sleeping the only thing we do in delta?

PRESENTER: No. Dreams, which occur during the rapid eye movement (REM) stage of sleep, are thought to occur at the high alpha, low beta, or possibly alpha or theta frequency. And we may do many other things during delta besides sleep; for example, some researchers believe that sleepwalking and out-of-body experiences, sometimes remembered as a dream, occur at delta. Much is yet to be learned about deep brain wave frequencies.

PARTICIPANT: What or which frequencies can help me most?

PRESENTER: You need them all and you use them all. For the purposes of learning, however, alpha should be the focus. I believe alpha offers the greatest benefits for the learning of new information, retention, and recall; stress management and relaxation; self-motivation; creativity; and problem-solving. . . .

PARTICIPANT: I am learning quite a lot. But I need time to digest it all.

PRESENTER: We will explore accelerated learning and its methods at the next session.

NOTES

#35 Resources

Education and Training Resources

Instructor training in accelerated learning techniques is available from a number of national organizations whose programs include courses and workshops (including foreign language training) in the use of accelerated learning methodology and skills for the improvement of learning and memory retention.

Sources available include:

1. Accelerated Learning Systems, Inc.
   Douglas and Terry Webb
   6193 Summit Trail
   Norcross, GA 30092
   404/446-3852
2. James Bowser, Vice President for Academic Affairs
   Hocking Technical College
   Route 1
   Nelsonville, OH 45764
   614/753-3591
   For specialized training in brain dominance/ learning styles assessment
3. Brain Dominance Institute
   Ned Herrmann, President
   2075 Buffalo Creek Road
   Lake Lure, NC 28246
   704/625-9153
   For specialized training in brain dominance/ learning styles assessment
4. Center for Accelerated Learning
   David Meier, Director
   1103 Wisconsin St.
   Lake Geneva, WI 53147
   414/248-7070

5. International Language Services, Inc.
   Karen Whitely, President
   3400 Rosedale, #279
   Dallas, TX 75205
   214/750-1664
6. Lozanov Learning Institute, Inc.
   Louis Buchsbaum, President
   5430-F Lynx Lane
   Columbia, MD 21044
   202/882-4000 or 301/596-6778
   For language training
7. Self-Study Systems
   Brian M. Morrissey
   131 Eleventh St., N.E.
   Washington, DC 20002
   202/544-3960
8. Nancy H. Omaha Boy,
   Vice President for Academic Affairs
   Reading Area Community College
   10 S. Second St., P.O. Box 1706
   Reading, PA 19603
   215/544-3960
9. Society for Accelerated Learning and
      Teaching, Inc.
   P.O. Box 1549, Welch Station
   Ames, IA 50010
   515/296-8055
10. SuperlearningTM, Inc.
    Suite 4-A
    17 Park Avenue
    New York, NY 10016
11. R.G. Swartz and Associates
    Management Impact Skills
    P.O. Box 7568
    Lancaster, PA 17604-7568
    717/299-5061

References: 43

Suggested Readings

12. Anderson RH: Selecting and developing media for instruction. New York: Van Nostrander Reinhold, 1976.

    An excellent primer for an overall orientation of the application of media to education and training.

13. Brain/Mind Bulletin. Los Angeles: Interfact Press.

    A publication disseminating synopses of brain/mind research findings from various fields, with implications and applications. Address: Interfact Press, Box 42211, 4717 N. Figueroa St., Los Angeles, CA 90042 (213/223-2500).

14. Education Resources Information Center (ERIC). Washington, DC: US Department of Education, US Government Printing Office.

    A resource of educational research articles offered by the National Institute of Education. Many university libraries house ERIC documents.

15. Gawain S: Creative visualization. New York: Bantam, 1978.

    An excellent source of additional techniques for wording affirmations for particular situations (see Section #14).

16. Institute of Noetic Sciences Newsletter. Sausolito, CA.

    The institute, a non-profit foundation, aims to broaden knowledge of the potential of the mind and consciousness and to apply such knowledge for the improvement of the quality of life. Address: Institute of Noetic Sciences, 475 Gate Five Road, Suite 300, Sausolito, CA

94965 (415/331-5650).

17. Journal of the Society for Accelerated Learning and Teaching. Ames, IA.
    A journal publishing educational research articles pertaining to accelerated learning. Address: Society for Accelerated Learning and Teaching, Inc. (SALT), P.O. Box 1549 Welch Station, Ames, IA 50010 (515/296-8055).
18. Van Gundy AB: Training your creative mind. Englewood Cliffs, NJ: Prentice-Hall, 1982.
    An excellent right-brain, skill development book of exercises in creativity. This work is helpful in assisting the development of imagery (see Section #12).
19. Vitale BM: Unicorns are real. Rolling Hills Estates, CA: Jalmar Press, 1983.
    An excellent right-brain, skill development book. It is useful in assisting the development of imagery and gives specific examples of using imagery in the teaching and learning of left-brain academic subject areas.
20. What works: Research about teaching and learning. Office of Educational Research and Improvement, U.S. Department of Education, 1986.
    A summary of research findings relevent to formal education in the U.S. The author believes this summary should be read by all school board directors, administrators, teachers, and parents concerned about their children's education. Topics include "Reading to Children" and "Discipline."
    Reprints may be obtained by writing to: Information Services, Office of Educational Research and Development, U.S. Department of Education, 1200 Nineteenth Street, NW, Washington, DC 20208-1403 (800/424-1616).

#36 References

1. Achterberg J: Imagery in healing: Shamanism and modern medicine. Boston: New Science Library, 1985.
2. Ainsworth E: Biological, psychological, and sociological factors in aging: Implications for education. Dissertation, Pennsylvania State University, Harrisburg, 1989;1-32.
3. Atkinson W: Lighting and office: Cost versus comfort. The Office 1989;110:78-80.
4. Benson H, Klipper MZ: The relaxation response. New York: Avon, 1975.
5. Benson H, Proctor WM: Beyond the relaxation response. New York: Berkley Books, 1984.
6. Birren F: Color psychology and color therapy. Secausus, NJ: Citadel Press, 1961.
7. Borysenko J: Getting back in control. New Age Journal 1987;(May-June):17-23.
8. Borysenko J, Rothstein L: Minding the body, mending the mind. Reading, MA: Addison-Wesley, 1987.
9. Bowser JM: Basic dominance — Quadratic information processing: A brain-related model. Columbus, OH: Vimach Associates, 1988.
10. Breaking the code of musicality. Brain/Mind Bulletin, Special Issue 1985;10(415):1-2.
11. Buzan T: Use both sides of your brain. New York: EP Dutton, 1983.
12. Buzan T: Use your perfect memory. New York: EP Dutton, 1984.
13. Capra F: The Tao of physics: An explanation of the parallels between modern physics and eastern mysticism, 2nd ed. New York: Bantam, 1983.

14. Charlesworth EA, Nathan RG: Stress management: A comprehensive guide to wellness. New York: Ballentine Books, 1984.
15. Dossey L: Beyond illness: Discovering the experience of health. Boston: New Science Library, 1984.
16. Eccles Sir J, Robinson DN: The wonder of being human: Our brain and our mind. Boston: New Science Library, 1985.
17. Einstein's brain may hold clues to nature of genius. Brain/Mind Bulletin 1985;10(6):1.
18. Federally-funded study shows imagery boosts learning, recall. Brain/Mind Bulletin 1984;10 (2):3.
19. Fincher J: The brain: Mystery of matter and mind. Washington, DC: US News Books, 1981.
20. Friedman M, Ulmer D: Treating Type A behavior and your heart. New York: Ballentine Books, 1984.
21. Halpern S, Savary L: Sound health: The music and sounds that make us whole. San Francisco: Harper and Row, 1985.
22. Hampden-Turner C: Maps of the mind. New York: Collier Books, 1982.
23. Hanna RG Jr: Business correspondence. July 13, 1990 and August 2, 1990.
24. Hayward JW: Perceiving ordinary magic: Science and intuitive wisdom. Boston: New Science Library, 1984.
25. Herrmann N: The creative brain. Lake Lure, NC: Brain Books, 1988.
26. James U: The Herrmann/Myers-Briggs connection. International Brain Dominance Review 1986;3(2):32-35.
27. Knowles M: The adult learner: A neglected species, 2nd ed. Houston: Gulf Publishing Co., 1978.

28. Long HB: Adult learning: Research and practice. Cambridge: Cambridge Book Co., 1983;38-70.
29. Loye D: The sphinx and the rainbow: Brain, mind, and future vision. Boston: New Science Library, 1983.
30. Luscher M, Scott I (trans. and ed.): The Luscher Color Test. New York: Pocket Books, 1969.
31. Meer J: The light touch. Psychology Today 1985;19(9):60-67.
32. Ornstein R, Sobel D: The healing brain: Breakthrough discoveries about how the brain keeps us healthy. New York: Simon and Schuster, 1987.
33. Ornstein R, Sobel D: Healthy pleasures. Reading, MA: Addison-Wesley, 1989.
34. Ornstein R, Thompson RF, Macaulay D (illus.): The amazing brain. Boston: Houghton Mifflin, 1984.
35. Ostrander S, Schroeder L, Ostrander N: Superlearning. New York: Dell Publishing, 1979.
36. Pelletier KR: Mind as healer, mind as slayer: A holistic approach to preventing stress disorders. New York: Dell Publishing, 1977.
37. Remen N: Healing and wholeness: Living well and dying well. Institute of Noetic Sciences Newsletter 1986;14(1):3-7.
38. Roederer JG: Physical and neuropsychological foundations of music: The basic questions. In: Music, mind, and brain: The neuropsychology of music. Clunes M (ed.). New York: Plenum Press, 1982;37-46.
39. Seyle H: Stress without distress. New York: Harper and Row, 1974.
40. Siegel BS: Love, medicine, and miracles. New York: Harper and Row, 1986.

41. Simonton OC, Matthews-Simonton S, Creighton JL: Getting well again. New York: Bantam, 1978.
42. Springer SP, Deutsch G: Left brain, right brain. San Francisco: WH Freeman, 1981.
43. Swartz RG: Self-accelerated learning skills: Music To Learn By. Lancaster, PA: RG Swartz and Associates, 1984.
44. Tame D: The secret power of music. New York: Destiny Books, 1984.
45. Taylor E: Subliminal communication: Emperor's clothes or panacea? Salt Lake City: Just Another Reality Publishing, P.O. Box 12419 Las Vegas, NE 89112.
46. Tyner R: Office lighting can affect your profits. The Office 1986;103:113-114.
47. Winson J: Brain and psyche: The biology of the unconscious. New York: Vintage Books, 1985.